D0341677

NO HOPE

WHY I LEFT THE GOP
(AND YOU SHOULD TOO)

Jimmy LaSalvia

Cofounder of GOProud

Skyhorse Publishing

Skyhorse Publishing books may be purchased in bulk at special discounts for sales promotion, corporate gifts, fund-raising, or educational purposes. Special editions can also be created to specifications. For details, contact the Special Sales Department, Skyhorse Publishing, 307 West 36th Street, 11th Floor, New York, NY 10018 or info@skyhorsepublishing.com.

Skyhorse® and Skyhorse Publishing® are registered trademarks of Skyhorse Publishing, Inc.®, a Delaware corporation.

Visit our website at www.skyhorsepublishing.com.

10 9 8 7 6 5 4 3 2 1

Library of Congress Cataloging-in-Publication Data is available on file.

Cover design by Brian Peterson
Cover photograph by: Paul Morigi

ISBN: 978-1-5107-0238-7
Ebook ISBN: 978-1-5107-0239-4

Printed in the United States of America

For my friend Chris Barron,
with much love and gratitude for traveling along part
of this political journey with me.

CONTENTS

INTRODUCTION

After spending most of my life and professional career as a conservative activist and openly gay Republican strategist, working in the trenches of the culture wars, I decided to leave the Republican Party. I made a public statement when I made that decision in 2014, and my announcement received a lot of media attention. Many of my friends from all those years in politics reached out to me when they saw those news stories on MSNBC, The Daily Beast, Politico, Time.com, ABC News–Yahoo News, and others to tell me that they didn't blame me for leaving the party. They knew all that I had been through in my efforts to help the GOP. Some of them even told me that they were considering leaving the Republican Party too.

This book is for them, and for all of the Republicans across the country who are thinking about leaving the GOP. It's also for all of those Americans who are tired of compromising themselves to conform to one side or the other in our broken two-party political system. I know that many people will relate to my story, and many more will be surprised at the lengths I was willing to go to help my political party of choice. They will come to realize, as I have, that there is just no hope that things will ever get better in the Republican Party. It's better to leave it rather than to participate in an untenable coalition or to prop up a broken institution. In real-estate terms, the GOP is a teardown. I came to realize that my efforts to help make our country better would be more effective working outside of the two-party system.

My story takes place at the intersection of culture and politics. My experiences deal with the most prominent cultural issues in politics in recent history: the issues relating to our innate human trait of sexual orientation. Issues affecting those of us who happen to be gay have been at the forefront of our national and worldwide political dialogue for the last forty years, especially in more recent years. Many in the conservative movement and the Republican Party have sought to use the force of government to halt cultural evolution in this area. I was at the center of the debate on those issues within the Republican Party for more than a decade, and I eventually determined that the GOP is culturally out of touch.

Culture is much bigger than politics. It's the essence of who we are and how we live our lives. Political issues that result when culture and politics intersect are different than other issues that we deal with in politics. Cultural issues are very, very different from things such as tax policy, or banking regulations, or trade, which are analytical in nature. Cultural issues deal with who we are and how we live, so they are very personal and carry a heavy emotional component with them. I often say that all politics is personal, but that's especially true with some issues more than others.

Culture changes and evolves over time. Those changes and that evolution result from experiences that we all share. Culture is also influenced by those different experiences unique to people who are like us, whether it's because of our national origin, race, gender, religion, sexual orientation, age, or other characteristics that make up who we are. Those unique experiences give us a point of view that may be different from others. Modern life in

America today includes people with many different points of view from many cultural backgrounds. Today in America, our shared cultural evolution recognizes our modern multicultural world and embraces it.

There is, however, a portion of America, mostly conservative Republicans, who resist participating in that shared cultural evolution. That's evident when issues relating to things such as race, gender, and sexual orientation are debated. This group wants to bring America back to a time when straight, white, Christian men dominated our culture, instead of modernizing and embracing new multicultural realities. These new realities include the fact that white people will be a minority in America by 2040.

I have a right-of-center perspective, but I've never thought that holding conservative principles and values meant that I had to live in the past. I've always tried to apply my principles and values to modern problems, while recognizing the reality that culture changes and evolves. I spent my career trying to help the Republican Party to evolve and become a modern party that is in touch with real life in America today, because I thought it was important to have a competitive right-of-center party in our closed two-party system. Real life in America today includes gay people, living their lives openly and honestly. America today also includes more diverse points of view than ever before, and all of those viewpoints should be represented in the political arena.

While my experiences dealt most directly with the issues relating to gay people in the Republican Party, I saw firsthand the way many other positions based in the past are holding the party back, too. Frankly, the party's handling of homosexuality alone renders it unacceptable in today's America, but the issue of sexual orientation is just the biggest example of a much broader problem. There are many examples on a variety of topics that show that the cultural disconnect on the right is just too severe to overcome.

There are big things, such as the way Republicans have talked about and dealt with the immigration crisis, birth control, and other big issues that easily demonstrate that there is a segment of the GOP who refuse to accept modern American life. My unique, behind-the-scenes perspective on some of the most prominent examples of the GOP's cultural disconnect has helped to amplify those small examples to me when I see them. As the cofounder of the prominent national organization for gay conservatives and their allies, GOProud, I worked with some of the biggest players in the conservative movement and Republican Party to help to build a coalition that included everybody, including gay people. I learned, firsthand, what they think and why they make the decisions they make.

I decided to write this book about my experiences and observations inside the conservative movement and Republican Party to demonstrate to all of those good people who think that the GOP is a viable option for them, that it's not. For all of those culturally modern people who think that they can change the party and help it to be more connected to our modern multicultural reality: there's no hope. Take it from me.

This story chronicles the lengths I went to in order to help the party, all while enduring attacks from forces across the political spectrum, from both the extreme right and the extreme left. I had hope, time and time again, that the GOP would change and evolve, but I was disappointed every time. The reality is that there is a segment of the GOP that is going to hold the party back and keep it from winning national elections again.

I used to think that the only way I could make an impact was to join one of the two parties and work within the system. I don't think that anymore, and I have decided to focus my efforts going forward on bringing reforms to the closed two-party system, so that everyone's point of view can be represented in American politics without having to be a part of one of the two major political parties.

I hope that after you read my story you will decide to take the bold first step, the one that I took, and reject partisan politics. I hope that you'll decide, as I have, that you can make a difference without compromising yourself to fit one political party or the other. Let us join together to work outside of the hopeless GOP and the broken two-party system to make our country better.

1

INDEPENDENCE

It was the evening before a conservative media conference, and a lot of the attendees were sitting and visiting in the hotel bar. A group of us decided to venture out of the hotel to get some dinner. We were trying to decide where to eat, and I suggested that we find some Indian food, or maybe a Thai restaurant. My suggestions were roundly rejected by the half-dozen or so in our group. "No, let's find some American food," one of them countered. "I don't eat any of that weird stuff." They weren't even willing to do something as simple as trying foods from other cultures. We ended up getting burgers and fries at a chain restaurant in a suburban shopping center, because that's what they were used to and comfortable eating.

A story about us debating which restaurant to eat at may seem petty and silly, but it was telling to me. Many on the right are so closed-minded and resistant to different people that they can't even bring themselves to try the food from different cultures! Honestly, it was the little things like that that put everything into context for me. Many people on the right really aren't comfortable outside of their own cultural experience, and they don't want to evolve, and in many cases they advocate for the government to pass laws to help them to keep the country from changing culturally.

The majority of Americans think that they are wrong, so many on the right spend a lot of time and energy defending conservative positions that are culturally out of touch. They defend to the extreme everyone's right to have an unpopular opinion on culture-related topics, even when those opinions cross the line into what is morally unacceptable. The reality is that popular opinions are most often popular because they are right. It's not that the majority of Americans are just pushing a radical politically correct agenda, as some conservatives would claim; it's that the majority has evolved to an opinion that is morally correct. That morally correct majority opinion is based on the cultural realities of the times. Many of those correct opinions evolved based on the question of harm. If someone is harmed by one position on an issue, then it's usually determined to be wrong. To formulate a morally correct position based on the question of harm requires the ability to empathize with others who aren't like you, to determine if they are harmed by your position. Evolution to a morally correct position that society accepts as right doesn't happen with every issue in politics, but it's important to recognize it when it does.

One recent example has been the public debate over popular sports teams' mascots. Many of those mascots were adopted a long time ago at a different point in our cultural evolution. Today, some of them are simply tacky and ignore modern realities, such as the continued use of the term "Redskins" as the mascot for Washington, DC's National Football League franchise. Culture has evolved to a point where we recognize that word as a derogatory term referring to Native Americans, now that the settlers aren't at war with them. Many on the right have defended the team's owners' "right to free speech" regarding their team's mascot, even though the term is disrespectful to others.

Now, I don't think that team owners should be forced by the government to change their mascots, or anything like that, but they should recognize that their mascot's name is unacceptable in the modern world. It's just wrong, and most Americans agree on that. Too many on the right spend too much time defending others' right to be wrong, eventually appearing to be wrong themselves, whether they actually hold the wrong opinion themselves or not. That's part of being a team player on our "us versus them" political landscape. Defend your team even when they are wrong.

I couldn't defend the Republican Party's right to be wrong anymore, because it was damaging to me. The cultural disconnect is just too severe. Compromising my integrity by staying on the team wasn't worth it for me. I could still hold on to my principles and my vision of government that included a strong national defense, support of the free market, and the other good positions of the team without being part of them.

The day I decided to leave the GOP, I was swimming in the city pool next to Eastern Market in the Capitol Hill neighborhood of Washington, DC, where I lived. It was the middle of the afternoon and I had the whole pool to myself. I felt like I was swimming in a great abyss. My experiences in politics over the last two decades were spinning in my head. My whole professional life was flashing before my eyes as if I were having a near-death experience.

When you work in politics, they tell you to pick a team and stick with it, because the parties make the rules and playing by their rules is the only way you'll get things done. I had done that for over twenty years as a Republican activist and political professional. I had stuck with a team that wasn't always happy to have me on it, because I am a gay person.

As I swam, I thought about the life I had lived as a team player in Republican politics. I remembered cheering Pat Buchanan's infamous anti-gay culture-war speech at the 1992 Republican National Convention, even though I knew that it was wrong, because I knew deep down that I was a gay person myself. I thought about how difficult it had been coming to terms with my own sexual orientation and thinking that I would never work in politics again because of it. I was pounding the water with every stroke, harder and harder, and getting more and more emotional thinking about the end of a career that, until now, I had been very proud of.

My goggles started to fill with tears as I relived the feeling of betrayal I felt when President George W. Bush used a divisive anti-gay strategy to drive anti-gay voters to the polls in his reelection effort in 2004. All politics is personal, and 2004 was as personal as it got for me. It motivated my decade-long work to try to change the Republican Party's anti-gay culture, and to try to help modernize it to save it from extinction.

The events of the last few years, when I led the national organization for gay conservatives that I cofounded, GOProud, were the memories that were most emotional for me during that swim. We had worked so hard to try to help the Republican Party and the conservative movement, but I had realized that despite all of the incredible victories we had in helping to build an inclusive coalition, we had ultimately failed because an ugly, intolerant segment of that coalition still wielded too much power. The most telling indicator had been a well-publicized three-year struggle to have our group be a sponsor of the annual Conservative Political

Action Conference (CPAC), ultimately ending in GOProud being banned from CPAC simply because we were gay. We had also confronted the reality of the power of the anti-gay folks during the 2012 presidential primary and, most significantly, during our time as the only national gay organization supporting the Republican nominee, Mitt Romney.

I had seen it up close and personal. There is still a segment of the GOP who just don't like people who aren't like them, and no matter how much work I did to make the party more inclusive, no matter what my success in helping conservatives to appear culturally connected, that intolerant group would continue to bring the whole thing down.

For too long, I tried to make that team better. While I tried not to compromise my principles, by aligning myself with people who exclude people who aren't like them, I was compromising myself. I always thought that I was doing something good, and certainly my intentions were good, but at the end of the day, it's not good to make bad people look good. That's what happens as long as all the good people in the conservative movement allow the bad ones to stick around, because enabling bigotry makes you a bigot, too.

Through lap after lap in the pool, I thought about all of the great victories I had had. I did things that had never before been done on the right to show that conservatives were modern, inclusive, and culturally connected. I was so proud of that, but it was frustrating to continue to see all that progress squashed by the fact that the bigots were still tolerated. I likened my work to that of a gardener who works hard to have the most beautiful rose garden. (I thought that I had done a lot to grow a lot of damn roses.) But no matter how many beautiful, sweet-smelling roses you grow, if you don't clean up the dog shit in your yard, then it's still going to stink.

Cultural evolution has always played a role in American politics. Slavery, women's suffrage, African American civil rights, the sexual revolution, women's liberation, and other cultural movements have all had an impact on policy and politics. Societal standards and norms change and evolve over time. When it comes to cultural issues in politics, it's likely that today's deeply held belief will become tomorrow's untenable position. Eventually, "right versus left" becomes "right versus wrong" in voters' minds.

It doesn't take long for some positions and views to make the politicians and political parties that hold them unacceptable to voters. We've seen it over and over again: political movements that fail to evolve will ultimately be left in the past. Remember the Dixiecrats? They were the political party that failed to evolve on issues relating to race, including racial segregation in the military and education, in the 1940s and '50s. That party no longer exists.

Most of my direct experience centered on the most recent prominent cultural shift, the societal acceptance of homosexuality. I spent over a decade working professionally as a gay Republican activist, first with the national staff of the organization for gay Republicans, Log Cabin Republicans, then leading the gay conservative organization I cofounded, GOProud. My activism took place on two fronts, both as a Republican Party activist, and also as part of the broader gay rights movement.

The once-fringe issue of gay rights matured into a major political movement with the AIDS epidemic in the 1980s. Evangelist Pat Robertson's presidential campaign in 1988 and the formation of the Christian Coalition and other organizations such as the Family Research Council marked the formalization of the national conservative effort to oppose the normalization of homosexuality. The culture war on that issue has raged ever since, and now, at its conclusion, the losing side has been greatly damaged. Their view has been rendered unacceptable by a majority of Americans.

While the rest of the country was moving on, the once broad-based social conservative movement began its own transformation. Other issues and traditional values took a backseat to their opposition to homosexuality and gay people. The third leg of Ronald Reagan's winning conservative coalition stool has become nearly exclusively an anti-gay industry. Their numbers are dwindling and it has ultimately become the GOP's Achilles' heel. In fact, a 2015 Gallup poll showed that the number of Americans who identify as socially conservative is at its lowest point in history, at only 31 percent. In other words, over two-thirds of America thinks that social conservatives are wrong.

Of course, that issue is the most personal and emotional for me, because I am a gay person, but there were other areas in which I found myself increasingly culturally out of step with the base of the GOP. More and more, I found myself disagreeing with "my team" on issues. Whether it was basic things such as government shutdowns and kicking people off of unemployment during Christmastime, or more substantive issues, I found myself on the other side more often than ever before. This was especially true when it came to cultural issues and issues that affect people personally.

One of the issues that disturbed me the most was immigration. After the 2012 election, the Republican National Committee conducted a review of their election loss, called The Autopsy, which had addressed Hispanic outreach and the political need for comprehensive immigration reform, but the GOP still refuses to seriously address the broken immigration system.

For me, it's not about the politics of the issue; it's a crisis that has to be addressed. Being a free-market person, I see it as a simple supply-and-demand issue. There are more people desiring to immigrate to the United States than there are visas available for them to do it legally.

Our border should absolutely be secure to prevent illegal activity and threats to our national security, but why are we keeping out good people who just want a better life for their families? Our immigration system today is so restrictive that many feel that they have no better option than to risk everything and immigrate here illegally. Why not just let them immigrate legally?

Too many on the right have been very harsh in their rhetoric and actions toward undocumented immigrants, and also toward the economic refugees that come across our southern border. I was sickened in 2014 to see the news reports on FOX News and other television networks of conservatives standing on the border, banging on school buses full of desperate children, screaming at them to go home. Have they forgotten who we are as Americans? Or maybe they have never truly embraced the American Dream and what it means to be American. We are a nation of immigrants.

The argument I usually hear against open immigration is that people will come from all over the world to take advantage of welfare and our government-provided social services. First, I don't know of anyone who aspires to that. Nobody's American Dream is welfare—it's opportunity. If access to social services is your argument against immigration, then let's put some rules in place regarding how long you have to have worked in this country before you can access them.

The other argument is that immigrants will take jobs away from American citizens. Bullshit. Increased immigration will only increase our talent pool and increase the demand for housing, consumer goods, services, etc., which will in turn create more jobs. You see, more people means more jobs. Look back at history. It's true. Immigration grows the economy.

I suspect that the Republicans' problem with immigration is that it's another issue that just boils down to the fact that there is a segment of the conservative movement and the Republican Party who just don't like people who aren't like them. Different language, different color skin, and just general cultural diversity make them uncomfortable. I know, from my personal experience, that gay people make many of them uncomfortable.

I've always considered myself to be staunchly pro-life when it comes to abortion, but my advocacy for public policy is based in reality. It's important, whatever the issue, that our policy proposals recognize the cultural and political realities of our times. I have traditional values, but I also have a vision of government that gives it a limited role in our lives. We need to recognize the reality that abortion is legal in this country. While there should be regulations to make sure it's safe, we should do most of the advocacy work outside of the purview of government if we want to reduce the number of abortions.

Even I was appalled a couple of years ago when the nation's eyes turned toward the Texas Legislature and the proposed extreme abortion regulations being offered as a way to close abortion clinics in that state. The regulations regarding abortion facilities, and the requirements that providers must meet, were so stringent that very few of the clinics in the state could comply with them. The whole episode gave a state legislator, Wendy Davis, national notoriety, and gave conservatives a bad name. It was an example of how it's never enough for the social conservatives. They push for the most extreme until they get what they want, no matter how it affects people or how it's perceived by the public. Perception is reality in politics.

As I swam those laps, I realized that I had held onto the conservative Republican label longer than I should have, because I thought that I needed the credibility of it to be able to help the right evolve. I realized that it was hopeless. They weren't going to evolve on gay rights or other cultural issues fast enough. America had moved much farther, much faster, and left the GOP behind. Now, coming to that realization, I could shed that label. I was free to shed the skin I wore in order to do a job I couldn't bring myself to do anymore.

It was snowing during my walk home from the pool that day. The snow was accumulating on the sidewalks, and I felt it crunch under my feet every time I took a step. With every crunch, I became more and more confident in my decision. This was a walk of resolution.

As soon as I got home, I downloaded the voter registration form from the Board of Elections website and changed my party affiliation to "No Party." Then I posted a photo of the form with a 294-word blog post on my website—a site that usually only attracted a couple of dozen visitors per day. This is what I said:

> *A new Gallup poll came out last week showing that a record number of Americans, 42%, reject both major political parties and identify as independent. Republicans are at a historic low of only 27%.*
>
> *I've said for a long time that both John McCain and Mitt Romney won independents, but lost the election, because most independents used to be Republicans. They were Republicans, but now they are too embarrassed to formally affiliate with a party that's lost its way.*

Today, I joined the ranks of unaffiliated voters. I am every bit as conservative as I've always been, but I just can't bring myself to carry the Republican label any longer. You see, I just don't agree with the big-government 'conservatives' who run the party now.

The other reason I am leaving is the tolerance of bigotry in the GOP. The current leadership lacks the courage to stand up to it—I'm not sure they ever will.

I have worked hard to help to create an atmosphere on the right where conservatives can openly support gay Americans and even support same-sex marriage. In that effort, we have won, but there is more work to do to root out the anti-gay and other forms of bigotry in the party.

So I changed my voter registration today —"No Party."

Things are changing, and I've been writing a lot about a recalibration that is happening in the political sphere these days. I'll share my thoughts on the changing political land-scape over the coming months and year on this site, and in a book I hope to complete this year.

So, now I feel a huge sense of freedom. I am an independent conservative. (That sounds much better than "gay Republican.")

That blog post attracted a ton of attention. When I woke up the next morning, I heard my decision to leave the GOP reported on MSNBC. That was just the tip of the iceberg of the media attention that would come my way.

Honestly, I really wasn't that surprised. I knew that my announcement would get a lot of press, because we had been so good at generating earned media with GOProud. What I didn't expect was the outpouring of support from other conservatives and Republican insiders. I was overwhelmed with private messages and emails, from everyone from grassroots activists to famous leaders on the right, telling me that they agreed with me. It really blew me away that some really big names reached out to me, such as the executive producer of the highest rated right-wing radio show, a former Republican National Committee chairman, several FOX News and other conservative media personalities, and lots of conservative leaders with whom I had worked in coalition over the years. I don't want to "out" all of those people here by name, because I want them to pay attention to the message of this book without drawing too much attention to them. Some said, "I'm right behind you." They wanted to leave too. Of course, many of them had way too much to lose professionally to turn on the team the way I had. Many of them make their living working in conservative politics. The messages that meant the most came from people who knew the stories of what I went through in my work, such as what went on behind the scenes with the CPAC sponsorship controversy.

Those 294 words in my blog post had an impact in the media, and they also had an impact with people. I had really struck a nerve. I heard over and over again about how people don't feel like either major political party represents them anymore. The media storm I was in and the reaction I received showed me that I had made the right decision. I also confirmed my membership of a new majority—a majority of Americans who are ready to leave the old two-party system behind.

Around that time, I was at a small dinner party. There were five of us at dinner: two women, their husbands, and me. All of us were about the same ages, in our early forties. Both women were working mothers in marketing and public relations, and their husbands had good jobs, one in IT consulting and the other in the defense industry. Both couples were white, educated, suburban-dwelling, middle- to upper middle-class families. They are all conservative, right of center in their political views.

We were having a discussion about the state of American politics. They were all just as fed up as I was with the Republicans. None of us felt like the Democratic Party was an option for any of us, because the Democrats are out of touch economically and have a vision of government that gives the government too big a role in our lives. We couldn't even decide what to call ourselves—Conservatives? Moderates? Liberals? Libertarians? Pragmatists? That's a situation that more and more Americans are finding themselves in. Most Americans now identify as independent, because they don't fit any of those traditional labels and neither major political party represents them.

I asked the group, "What do you call people who believe that the government should live within its means and not tax us anymore, protect us from the bad guys, preserve America as a beacon of freedom in the world, allow for a competitive free market, and leave us the hell alone in our personal lives?"

One of the women responded, "Normal people."

That's it! Normal people! Obviously, that's an oversimplified vision of the role of government, but we all had the sense, in broad terms, of what the government's role should be. The reason there was such a positive reaction to my announcement that I was leaving the GOP is that there are just a whole lot of "normal people" in this country.

I should have broken free and become politically independent a long time ago. Everyone has the natural desire to fit in and be a part of a group. We all have to work to overcome that desire to fit in, in order to see that being a freethinker is better.

While I never said or did anything I didn't believe in, I certainly kept many of my dissenting opinions to myself and cheered at the top of my lungs when I fell in line with the team's groupthink. I've thought about all the times in my political messaging when I turned up the volume on some things, and turned down the volume on others, trying to make sure that my audience in the party was pleased, and that I fit in on the team. I certainly did that sometimes when it came to issues relating to gay people. I often downplayed my support for marriage equality, while trumpeting my position in favor of Second Amendment rights. That position was more accepted among the other conservative Republicans. I don't really regret doing any of that because, as you'll learn, I was doing it with a specific mission in mind, but I do wish that I had given myself permission to say exactly what I thought sooner.

That feeling of independence and choice is something I had been searching for. That is what most new independents find joy in—an ability to make an intelligent decision rather than a biased one.

When I left my job as the executive director of GOProud, I went to visit a friend, Rich Tafel, one of the only people I could think of who had been as deep into the belly of the beast as I had and had confronted the bigotry in the Republican Party in a revolutionary way. Rich had been head of Log Cabin Republicans, a gay Republican group, during the 1990s. He helped to establish that organization to give gay Republicans a voice in national politics in Washington. I needed someone to talk to, and I knew that Rich had been through his own type of journey as a theologian who had worked in the political arena.

We visited for a while on the rooftop patio of the Newseum Building in downtown Washington, where Rich lives. I told him about my decision to leave GOProud, and my realization that no matter what we did, the bigots would still be tolerated in the GOP. He listened to my emotional rant. Then Rich asked me, "How are you treating your wounds?"

My eyes welled up with tears and my lower lip began to tremble because I knew that he knew exactly what I was feeling. Then he gave me some advice. He told me to release all of the anger and resentment I had inside after years of working in the trenches. He said those feelings wouldn't serve me going forward. I knew he was right, but that's easier said than done. He said, "You have traveled a long road, now make sure to take care of yourself."

Now I knew that the free and inspired feeling I felt when registering for "No Party" was an indication of the healing that Rich had talked about a few months earlier. I was relieved to have found it.

Rich was right. I had traveled a long, tough road.

2

BORN THIS WAY

I often say that I was born gay and I was born conservative. I don't remember a time when I didn't have a generally conservative point of view and—until recently—identify with the Republican Party, once I knew what that was. I grew up in an Air Force family during the height of the Cold War. I always remember my dad, who was a navigator and offensive systems officer on B-52s and then B-1 bombers, talking about the bad guys he was trained to protect us from. So my whole life has always been in the context of "us versus them." We're the good guys, and they're the bad guys. The first president I remember was President Ford, but the first election I remember paying attention to was President Reagan's election in 1980. We lived on the Air Force base in Georgia where President Carter would land Air Force One when he would go to his home in Plains. I remember seeing Air Force One and President Carter once when they took a bunch of us from the base elementary school out to the flight line to see him arrive. My parents were for Reagan, and so were most of their friends. Of course, on the base where we lived, it seemed that almost everyone was for Reagan because, like my parents said, he was pro-military and Carter wasn't.

So I was a child of the Reagan Revolution, growing up on Air Force bases all over the country. When I was fifteen years old, we moved to western South Dakota, to Ellsworth AFB in the Black Hills. The teenage years are when you start to figure out what you think. The mountain west libertarian-conservatism that was the dominant thinking in western South Dakota really resonated with me. The reliance on the individual and on each other before turning to the government is a principle that remains strong there, probably because of the pioneering heritage of the area. Once you set out for the Dakota Territory with your wagon train in the 1880s, you were all on your own. That mindset is still very much part of the culture there.

It seemed like common sense for the government to live within its means and to make sure people kept as much of their money as possible to reinvest in the economy. The main job of the federal government was to protect us from the bad guys, which is what my dad did, and we needed to make that a priority in spending. I grew to have a vision of a limited role for government. Let's approach every problem with the question: how can we solve this problem on our own, without the government's involvement? Only if that won't work should we look at solutions that require government involvement.

One important role of the government is to keep us safe in a dangerous world. I have never thought that the isolationist, non-engagement views that many liberals hold recognize the reality of the national security threats we face. I have always favored views of conservatives that include an engaged foreign policy that protects and promotes America's role as the beacon of freedom for the world.

By the early 1990s, I was a full-fledged Republican activist and a professional staffer on campaigns in South Dakota. I was part of the youth program at the 1992 Republican National Convention, I led my local College Republicans club, and I eventually worked for the speaker of the state House and then the governor.

It was during my time in South Dakota in my mid-twenties that I came to terms with my own sexual orientation and with homosexuality in general, along with most of the rest of the country. On television, shows like Ellen DeGeneres's groundbreaking sitcom *Ellen*, *Will and Grace*, and later *Queer Eye for the Straight Guy* brought "normal" gay people into homes across America. Before then, the only gay people most people saw on TV were the most flamboyant ones who appeared in news coverage of pride parades or the people in stories about the AIDS crisis. These pop culture indicators on television showed that the country was coming to accept gay Americans as mainstream members of society.

The 1990s was when I began to recognize the cultural realities of real life in America. While I have always considered myself a traditional social conservative, instead of focusing on using the government to create a "perfect" society, I began to see a more limited, libertarian role for government. On issues such as abortion, drugs, and some other cultural issues, I started to recognize that focusing energy and resources outside of the scope of government was a more effective way to affect culture. Using the force of government to implement social policy denies societal evolution, and it turns the government against people, or at least some people in some ways. It's better to influence the culture than the government on those types of issues. I also grew to oppose government-based efforts to pick winners and losers, such as tax breaks and incentives, in order to encourage one behavior over another. Everyone should be treated the same under the law.

My vision of government was consistent with Republican principles, but it appeared that I was drifting from the views of many other Republicans. Many of the activists I worked with in South Dakota, and later in Kentucky, held on to their hardcore socially conservative views and their government-focused strategy for achieving their goals. They wanted to use the government to achieve their socially conservative utopia. For a while I thought that I was growing out of touch, because I used to agree 100 percent with them. I started to feel odd, like my perspective was out of the mainstream, but I realized it wasn't. They were the ones who were out of the mainstream. It was my evolution on homosexuality, confirmed by those pop culture markers that showed that the country was coming to terms with gays, that was a key—albeit very personal—indicator to me that I was actually in touch culturally.

True to form, whenever cultural standards and norms change, politicians and political parties are usually the last to publicly acknowledge it. We saw that during the civil rights struggle, and that's certainly been the case with the "gay issue," too. By the 1990s, though, there was a definitive split starting to emerge between the Democrats and the Republicans on gay rights.

The difference in tone and maturity between the major political parties was seen in the parties' conventions in 1992. The Democrats featured Barbara Jordan using lines like, "This party will not tolerate bigotry under any guise . . ." and "We seek to unite people, not divide them." Whereas the Republican convention that year will forever be remembered for Pat Buchanan's famous "culture-war speech." I remember that Buchanan speech like it was yesterday. I was a twenty-one-year-old College Republican from South Dakota, in the beginning stages of my political career. I stood in the crowd on the convention floor chanting, "Family rights forever, gay rights never!" I did that because that's what everyone else was doing, but it didn't feel right. Deep down I knew that I was gay, even though it would be some years before I would come to accept it. I was chanting to show that I thought like the others in my party. I pretended to agree that gays are harmful to America. I certainly didn't understand how that display must have been received by television viewers at home.

As the Christian Coalition and other groups helped the GOP ramp up the culture wars, the Democrats began to bridge the divide. The Dems began to attract moderate and even some conservative voters who were turned off by harsh rhetoric on the right. Democratic President Bill Clinton, a culturally connected, fiscally conservative "New Democrat," had eight years in the White House. The Democrats had previously turned off most voters, including me, by being culturally extreme and fiscally irresponsible. Most conservatives had an image of a typical Democrat as a hippie "San Francisco liberal" who was hell-bent on growing the government and providing government handouts to lazy "welfare queens." Clinton was successful in rebranding his "New" Democratic Party as more fiscally responsible and culturally connected with life in 1992.

I didn't buy all of Clinton's sales pitch. I was still on board with the GOP, but after seeing President Clinton be the first president to really publicly embrace the gay community, in recognition of the fact that gay people were part of life in America now, I was worried that the Republicans were never going to get it. As the religious activists—such as Jerry Falwell, Pat Robertson, and the Christian Coalition's Ralph Reed—on the right exerted more and more power to keep the Republicans trapped in the past, I feared that the party would be lost for good. Although Clinton signed the Defense of Marriage Act (DOMA) and Don't Ask, Don't Tell (DADT) laws that did great damage to gay Americans, his rhetoric and attitude toward gays, mostly by using the platform of the presidency to publicly engage with and embrace the gay community, reflected progress that the GOP didn't have. Most in the Republican Party were still actively campaigning against and voicing opposition to homosexuality.

In 1996, after working on several campaigns in South Dakota, I was out of college and without a job. I decided to look for work in Louisville, Kentucky, where my family is from. It's a large city and I thought there would be more opportunities for employment there. I was also coming to terms with my sexual orientation, and I just didn't think that work in Republican politics in South Dakota would be an option for me. I knew that a traditional political path of elected office or an appointed position was never going to be an option for an openly gay conservative from a red state. The anti-gay opposition would have prevented that. I ended up finding a job in the development office at Kentucky Opera. I had never even been to an opera before, but I thought, well, I'm gay now. I guess I'll work at the opera instead of in Republican politics! So I was out of politics and on the sidelines in Kentucky for the last four years of the Clinton administration, but even a casual politically aware observer like me could see the impact that a president from a southern state was having on political attitudes toward gays.

Clinton had an impact in other cultural areas, too. Most significantly, he showed his willingness to stand up to the out-of-touch extremists in his party, as in his famous "Sister Souljah moment," when he denounced the racist comments of African American political activist and hip-hop artist Sister Souljah. That was a key public repudiation of racism among a segment of the black community and that extreme segment of the Democrats' coalition. It served to disassociate Clinton and his party from that segment, enabling him to begin to build a new Democratic brand that was in touch with where the country was culturally.

While Clinton was standing up to the extremists in his party in the 1990s, Republicans were doing the opposite. The extremists on the right were driving the agenda and they solidified the GOP's reputation for intolerance. For example, Senator Jesse Helms (R-NC) ran his race-baiting "Willie Horton" ads against his black opponent Harvey Gantt in his reelection campaign in 1996. There were many efforts by state-level Republican politicians to display the Ten Commandments and fly Confederate flags at public buildings. There were also continued, sustained anti-gay politics on the right throughout the decade.

No Republican standard-bearer has ever had the courage to stand up and forcefully repudiate the extremists in the conservative coalition, because the extremists have continued to make up a significant portion of the party. While there have been attempts to move away from extremist positions on the right, there has never been a "Sister Souljah moment" that casts out any part of the GOP's traditional coalition. Extremism has been tolerated in an effort to keep the extremists' votes, without regard to how many votes they may be driving away.

One example of the GOP inching toward the mainstream happened in 2000. I was excited and hopeful when then Texas Governor George W. Bush ran his campaign for president on what he called "compassionate conservatism." He recognized that the party was perceived as intolerant and uncaring about people who aren't like them. It was encouraging to think that there was a conservative who cared about people, and understood that every political issue is personal to someone. I thought Republicans might just understand how political issues impact the daily lives of average Americans, even if they weren't straight, white, Christian conservatives. This was an opportunity for the GOP to show the country that they got it.

The phrase "compassionate conservatism" did strike me as a bit condescending, though. After all, aren't you supposed to have compassion for those less fortunate than you? Rather than a message of something like "we are all in this together, everyone, no matter who you are, let's all pull together," I felt that "compassionate conservatism," rang a tone of moral superiority, but I thought it was a good start at showing some personal connection from the right.

Part of the Bush "compassionate conservative" campaign strategy included an attempt at gay outreach. Arizona Senator John McCain had had more prominent gay Republicans supporting him in the primary that year, but the Bush campaign, after refusing to meet with the Log Cabin Republicans, did eventually put forth some effort to engage with gay voters after the primary. After he secured the nomination, Bush hosted a meeting with twelve gay Republicans in Austin, Texas. That group became known as the "Austin 12." Bush emerged from the meeting with the Austin 12 and said that he was a "better person" for having had the conversation with them. Again, I thought that was a bit condescending, but it was progress. Of course, there was an important segment of the GOP, the anti-gay faction, that was outraged that he would even take the meeting.

The Austin 12 were instrumental in helping Bush with his messaging and how he phrased things regarding gay people. They also helped make history by requesting that a prominent, openly gay Republican address the 2000 Republican National

Convention in Philadelphia, with the result that Congressman Jim Kolbe (R-AZ) was given a speaking role on one evening during the convention. It may seem silly to think that giving a gay person a speaking role was a big step but it was a big deal to have a gay person step onto the Republican stage in primetime.

I was there the night Kolbe spoke to the convention about US trade policy. It was a huge moment of pride for every gay person in the convention hall, and also for many Republicans who were glad to see the party begin to try to move on from its anti-gay past. But one thing couldn't be ignored, and it ruined any display of progress that came from Kolbe's speech: Texas delegates, who were seated right down in the front because Bush was from Texas, and some other delegates scattered throughout the convention hall, turned their backs to Kolbe and/or bowed their heads as if to pray. It was a "prayerful protest." It was disgusting. The message that would be sent to the country was the opposite of what it should have been. The country didn't see compassionate, inclusive conservatives; they saw judgmental people who didn't respect anyone who wasn't like them. Their intolerance stained the entire convention.

The self-righteous protesting delegates didn't understand the negative message their actions were sending to the country, or maybe they just didn't care. The truth is, even if people agree with specific policy positions, nobody likes displays of ugliness or disrespect toward others, no matter how righteous the cause may or may not be.

★

The sad truth is that the speech by Congressman Kolbe in 2000 was the last time an openly gay Republican has addressed a Republican National Convention. Kolbe was also the last openly gay Republican to serve in Congress. He did not seek reelection in 2006. Nobody has ever been elected to Congress for the first time as an openly gay Republican. Both Kolbe and former Wisconsin Congressman Steve Gunderson, the first openly gay Republican member of Congress, came out as gay after they were already serving. Gunderson was outed in 1994 on the House floor by then Congressman Bob Dornan, a rabidly anti-gay Republican. Kolbe came out in 1996 when he learned that his sexual orientation would likely be reported in the gay magazine *The Advocate* after his vote in favor of the Defense of Marriage Act (DOMA). Several other Republican former members of Congress publicly came out as gay after they left Congress. None of the three openly gay Republicans who ran for Congress in 2014 won their elections, even though there was a "GOP wave." Those gay GOP nominees didn't win in 2014, in part, because anti-gay social conservative organizations including the National Organization for Marriage, the Family Research Council, and Focus on the Family urged their supporters in those districts not to support the Republican candidates because they were gay.

After Bush won the 2000 election, he went on to populate his administration with a lot of gay people, including appointing an openly gay man, Michael Guest, as US ambassador to Romania. Clinton's appointment of an openly gay ambassador had been very controversial with the American public, but Bush's move was not—a sign that the country was continuing to evolve. I had a lot of friends in the administration, and the Log Cabin Republicans had unprecedented access to the White House and a good relationship with the Republican National Committee. I went to the Log Cabin conference in 2002 and remember being pleasantly surprised that so many administration and party officials were part of the program. All those signs of positive progress were frowned upon by the social conservatives, and were a sign that Bush "got it."

I was getting excited about politics again and wanted to get back into it professionally. I had left the opera job by then and was working as a real estate broker in Louisville. I wasn't exactly sure how to transition back into politics, but I was definitely heading in that direction. It looked as though the Republican Party might be evolving just like I had, albeit a bit behind the rest of the country. It was 2002 and I hadn't worked professionally in politics since 1996. The new direction of the GOP gave me hope, and I began to think that working in politics would again be possible for me.

I was ready to rejoin the team and fight the other side again. I started to volunteer for candidates in Kentucky, including making calls and distributing literature for US Senator Mitch McConnell's reelection campaign that year.

In 2004, the Bush reelection campaign reversed their 2000 attempts at inclusion and compassion, and decided to use gay people as a target for the ugliest campaign tactic on the presidential level since the 1960s race-baiting "Southern strategy" used by the Nixon campaign. Ironically, then closeted gay Ken Mehlman, implementer of the Bush campaign strategy, apologized in a speech to the NAACP for the Republicans' history of exploitation of racial conflicts for political gain after he became RNC chairman.

That year, the Republican Party orchestrated the placement of proposed constitutional amendments banning gay marriage on the ballots in eleven states, including my state of Kentucky, in hopes of driving anti-gay evangelical voters to the polls in

November. President Bush also used the bully pulpit of the White House to advocate for an amendment to the US Constitution banning civil marriage for gay couples. It would have also banned civil unions. It was such an extreme measure that even President Bush, since he left office, has expressed regret for the way it all played out, though he has not backed away from his position on marriage.

Many other high-profile gay people have written and spoken about how the 2004 Bush campaign's attacks on gays felt to them. "A punch in the gut" is a common description of the feeling that many of us had. That's certainly how I felt. Is there anything our government should do that would cause that reaction by any of its citizens? Think about that. Is there anything that the government should do that would make millions of Americans feel like they had been punched in the gut?

This was more personal and motivating than anything I had experienced before in politics. I needed to take action. The president of the United States wanted to write discrimination against me into the United States Constitution. 2004 was a really tough time for me. It felt like it was the United States of America and the Commonwealth of Kentucky against Jimmy.

I knew at the time, and many other Republican activists knew, that the result of the president's strategy would do great long-term damage to the party. (Of course, they haven't won the White House since.) The polls showed that Americans overwhelmingly opposed civil marriage for gay couples, but what most polls didn't track was how many Americans opposed homosexuality. "Believing in homosexuality" is not like believing in the Tooth Fairy, or some other fantasy; it's a real thing in nature. Opposing homosexuality is like opposing rain— you can't. What has happened in our country over the last few decades is that almost everyone now recognizes that. The problem in 2004 for Republicans was that a large part of their base didn't separate their opposition to homosexuality from their opposition to same-sex marriage. The bigger problem for the GOP now is that many of them still don't. Even worse for them is that opposition to same-sex marriage is now an unacceptable position, too.

The 2004 strategy signaled to a generation of conservative operatives and commentators that wedge-issue, culturally divisive politics works. Many of them have taken it to another level in recent years on gay issues, women's issues, immigration, and other cultural issues. The Bush 2004 anti-gay strategy was the linchpin that let loose the politics of division that permeates the political landscape today.

By spring 2004 I knew that it was time for me to engage again, so I reached out to the folks at Log Cabin Republicans in Washington, DC, and set out to start a new Log Cabin chapter in Kentucky. It was slow going at first, but there was a climate on the ground in Kentucky that made recruitment easy. Many other conservatives, gay and straight, with views like mine wanted to help. The anti-gay politics happening in Washington and closer to home in Frankfort, the Kentucky state capital, meant that the days of standing on the sidelines were over for me and other fair-minded Republicans. It was time for me to stand up and give gay conservatives a voice in Kentucky.

The scene in the state capital of Frankfort was horrible. The state GOP leaders in the legislature, following directions from Bush strategist Karl Rove and, more importantly for them, Kentucky Senator Mitch McConnell, set out to place an anti-gay marriage constitutional amendment on the ballot in November. The tension in the capitol building during the couple of days I was there felt as though tempers could erupt any minute. There were protests and demonstrations on both sides of the gay marriage issue.

The anti-gay protestors used religion, their fundamentalist version of Christianity, to defend their anti-gay positions. They weren't all peaceful in their protests, either. It never happened to me, but gay friends of mine were spat on, and one was even hit by a Bible hurled at him in the Capitol rotunda. The religion-based attacks there, in capitals across the country, and in Washington shouldn't happen in a country like ours. That's what happens in third-world theocracies far, far away, not in our country.

The Republicans and the Christians—two identities I wore proudly—were the people responsible for this ugliness. This measure was antithetical to what I, and many normal Republican people, thought limited-government conservatives believed. My religion was about love. I didn't see love in the faces of any of the "Christian" protesters. My political party supposedly stood for expanding freedom, and this amendment limited my freedom. Rather than quit, I made the decision to fight to change the religious zealots in the party. I would help them to evolve the way I had.

Of course the anti-gay marriage amendment was on the ballot in Kentucky in November 2004, and I knew that there was more than enough support to pass it. While I led our local Log Cabin efforts to oppose the marriage amendment, I focused most of our efforts on helping a few local candidates whom I knew to be friendly to Log Cabin's pro-gay-rights mission. For example, there was a long debate over an LGBT-inclusive anti-discrimination ordinance in the city of Louisville, where I lived, and it was an issue in several of the local races that fall. Our Log Cabin group made phone calls and walked precincts on behalf of the Republican Metro Council members who supported the ordinance.

★

One night in the fall of 2004 I was making calls with a couple of Log Cabin folks on behalf of Louisville Metro Councilwoman Ellen Call at the local Republican "victory" office. It was a large call center in a suburban office park. That's where most GOP get-out-the-vote offices are located in any given city, because many older, white, suburban volunteers are often afraid to go down-town in the evenings, because they fear that they'll be victims of "crime" downtown. (I know that sounds crazy, but it's true.) I was annoyed because the information table there had brochures advo-cating for passage of the state marriage amendment. We were in an office set up to support Republican nominees for public office, not nonpartisan issue campaigns. There was no doubt that the anti-gay effort was an official Republican Party strategy.

I brought my concern to the congressional district GOP chair-woman, DeAnna Brangers, who was also the person in charge of the call center. I'll never forget what she said to me. It's burned in my memory. "You need to learn about political realities, Jimmy. The political reality is that being against gay marriage is a winner for Republicans. Karl Rove and the Bush campaign want us to distribute this literature because it's a winning issue for us. That's the political reality. Deal with it."

Now, that political reality has reversed, and opposition to same-sex marriage is a losing issue. In fact, the issue of marriage equality has moved farther and faster than anyone involved in that 2004 campaign could have ever imagined. I wonder how DeAnna and the others who implemented that strategy are deal-ing with that modern reality.

I ramped up my activism after the 2004 election. I was determined to save my GOP team from the disastrous path it had chosen. In 2006, I moved to Washington, DC, to work full-time in the national office of Log Cabin Republicans. It was a big step for me to make the move to Washington. This was the big time, and I wasn't sure I was ready. The state-level politicians and political hangers-on, like DeAnna Brangers, hadn't been easy to deal with. I wasn't sure how I would handle the bigger stage and bigger characters on the national level.

One thing that I learned early on in Washington is that there are actually very few "true believers" in the anti-gay, hard-core cultural politics of the right in Washington. There were a lot fewer anti-gay zealots than I had seen on the state level in Kentucky and South Dakota. Most people in Washington didn't seem to care about gay marriage, abortion, or other cultural issues; it was all about the politics of the issues for them. They knew that there was a segment of the party across the country that really, really cared about that stuff, so they played to that audience for votes, even though they truly didn't share that point of view.

Having failed in 2004, 2006, and 2008, the Republicans again attempted, and again failed, to pass the Federal Marriage Amendment in Congress. It was steadily losing support there and across the country, but some felt that introducing it and forcing votes on it would help Republicans politically. The staffs and even some of the members were disgusted by the strategy. Privately, they'd tell you exactly what they thought of the "crazies" among them, but when it came down to it, most of the members fell in line and supported the measure every time it was up for a vote. A common word in the vernacular of the professional Republican operatives in Washington is the "crazies."

That refers to the social conservatives, who are the ones who drive the anti-gay agenda.

By 2008, it seemed possible that the GOP's presidential nominee would be more inclusive in his rhetoric and policies than Bush had been in 2004. Fortunately, John McCain was, sort of. He had opposed the Federal Marriage Amendment, and had always been someone with whom Log Cabin could work. Even when he didn't agree with us on policy, he was more inclusive than most of the Republicans in Congress. Many of Log Cabin's members had supported McCain in 2000 and would do so again in 2008.

McCain hadn't been my first choice in the presidential primary in 2008. I supported former New York City Mayor Rudy Giuliani, and I wasn't the only one. In fact, Giuliani had so many gays supporting him that many in politics were calling him the "gay candidate," which certainly didn't help him in the GOP primary. He had a very inclusive record as mayor, and the fact that he temporarily lived with friends of his, who happen to be a gay couple, while he was going through a divorce was widely reported and endeared him to many gay Republicans. The anti-gay, out-of-touch segment of the party actively opposed him, and he never gained traction. It was disappointing that Giuliani hadn't done well, but it could have been much worse for gays if McCain hadn't won. We could have ended up with former Arkansas Governor Mike Huckabee as the nominee. He was an extremely anti-gay social conservative who also had a record of raising taxes and spending in his state. We couldn't have supported him because he was bad culturally and economically! We had long, tortured conversations at Log Cabin about the possibility of Huckabee or another crazy being the nominee. There were real questions about Log Cabin's ability to survive if the party nominated a hardcore social conservative again.

The worst-case scenario, though, would have been former Massachusetts Governor Mitt Romney as the nominee or even as the vice-presidential nominee. Romney had been an inclusive governor, but reversed himself on LGBT-inclusive non-discrimination laws and gays in the military in his 2008 presidential run. He also reversed his previously pro-choice position on abortion. He even went silent with his formerly inclusive rhetoric in order to pander to the fringe of the party. He had done aggressive gay outreach in his run for governor, including having campaign booths at gay pride events in Massachusetts in 2002. In his 2008 presidential campaign, the only outreach his campaign did was to the anti-gay social conservative constituency in the Republican Party. The message a Romney nomination would send others in the party would have been devastating—that you can't succeed in this party unless you reverse progress on issues affecting gay people, and go hardcore socially conservative. That would have greatly accelerated the GOP's cultural backslide that began in 2004. Log Cabin ran ads against Romney in Iowa and New Hampshire and we expressed our opposition to him and did a ton of media interviews about it.

It was a relief when McCain finally secured the nomination, but of course, the crazies didn't trust him. So even though he had an inclusive record and tone, he went about pandering to the hardcore social conservatives in hopes they wouldn't abandon the GOP in November. The best example of this was his selection of then Alaska Governor Sarah Palin as his running mate. McCain's top choices for the job, such as Senator Joe Lieberman (D-CT), Governor Jodi Rell (R-CT), and others, weren't from the social conservative wing of the GOP, and the campaign feared losing social conservative votes with a pro-choice running mate.

The Palin pick was initially seen as a win-win for the campaign. She demonstrated a level of McCain's cultural awareness because, of course, she was a woman. And she kept the crazies happy because she was a staunchly pro-life evangelical Christian. It was later in the 2008 campaign, when she "went rogue" and strayed from McCain campaign talking points, that she showed that her views were outside the mainstream. She demonstrated her own cultural disconnect and unpreparedness for national office during several interviews with mainstream media and social conservative media outlets, including Focus on the Family's James Dobson's radio program. The win-win pick ended up being a disaster.

Log Cabin had a great relationship with the McCain campaign. While he was pandering to the anti-gay crowd, he was also making an effort to reach out to gay voters. The campaign sent surrogates to Log Cabin events during the GOP convention, and we even helped with a McCain interview with the gay newspaper *The Washington Blade*—a first for a Republican presidential nominee—which showed the party the importance of reaching out and engaging with all demographic groups, even the gays. At the end of the day, McCain's positive progress was canceled out by the anti-gay pandering. Trying to have it both ways like that was like trying to split a baby, really.

In the end, I don't think there were very many who really thought that Democratic nominee Barack Obama would lose to McCain. Of course, there were times during the campaign when I thought McCain might pull it out and beat Obama, but it was time for a black president. Like every other cultural issue, when it's time, it's time. We've now seen it happen with race, soon for gender, and I work toward the day when it will happen for sexual orientation. Someday it will be time for a gay president, too.

3

THE TEA PARTY

There was a battle within the Republican Party after that 2008 election. Honestly, it's a battle that continues today. It's the battle between the culturally modern Republicans and the "socially conservative" Neanderthals who refuse to accept current standards and norms. Some in the party thought that John McCain was too socially moderate to be elected president, even though he took the most conservative positions on the issues the social conservatives cared about, and others argued that he was too conservative for the majority of Americans to feel comfortable with. That argument shaped the epic race for chairman of the Republican National Committee. The race featured several very socially conservative candidates, including former Ohio Secretary of State and Family Research Council Fellow Ken Blackwell, and several more inclusive figures, such as the eventual winner, former Maryland Lieutenant Governor Michael Steele. My former Log Cabin colleague, political consultant Chris Barron, and I decided to attend the RNC's meeting where the chairman election was taking place.

Chris and I were ideologically aligned and we shared a common strategic vision, too. He's one of the smartest people I've ever met in politics. Chris is a message man. He instinctively knows how to communicate to a determined audience better than anyone I've ever worked with. He doesn't need focus groups or polls; he just knows the right thing to say and how to say it. The day I met him in 2005, he complimented me on "always staying on message." Staying on message was especially important in our line of work, because gay conservatives never had a ton of money, people, or votes to deliver. All we had was our message, and Chris was the best at it.

The RNC meeting was held in Washington, DC, at the Capitol Hilton Hotel just down the street from the White House. Chris and I sat in the visitor section and watched the members of the RNC cast multiple rounds of votes for chairman. The whole time I was posting updates and commentary on Facebook and Twitter. There were tons of gay conservatives following and commenting on my updates. That wasn't that surprising, considering that approximately 1.4 million gay people voted for John McCain in the last election. There were a lot of us out there. Log Cabin was mired in debt and basically out of business now, having layed off its entire staff. Gay conservatives had no real representation in Washington.

Chris began making the case to me that we should start a new organization representing gay conservatives, with me as the executive director. I resisted at first. I just didn't know if I had it in me to start an organization from scratch. Personally, I needed money to live on, and fast. I knew that building a donor base that could support a full-time staff took time, sometimes even years. I didn't have that kind of time. Then a couple of things happened that helped to bring me around to Chris's point of view.

Michael Steele had been elected chairman that day, and a few weeks later he did or said something, I don't remember what it was exactly, that demonstrated his commitment to building a modern and diverse Republican Party. Chris called me and suggested that we put out a news release praising Steele. It was just two guys releasing a statement as "prominent gay Republicans." The audacity of that proposition clearly didn't faze us, because we did it. Frankly, we were a little surprised that the press release was picked up by several news outlets. It was becoming clear that there was space on the playing field for a new organization to be a national voice for gay conservatives.

Around that same time, President Obama gave his first speech to a joint session of Congress. I took to Twitter to broadcast some of my observations and reactions, mostly about what people in the audience were doing or what they were wearing. I said something about the jewelry worn by a young student who was in the audience because she had written a letter to the president. I said she was the only one in the room who knew how to accessorize! That tweet ended up in a *New York Times* story the next morning with tweets from famous political people. The headline was, "What they were saying during the speech." I was surprised, because I didn't know that anyone was reading my Twitter feed. I certainly didn't realize that my voice was influential enough to be included in the *New York Times!*

I was warming up to the idea of starting a new organization, but we had to be smart about it. We had the opportunity to start from scratch, so we needed to learn from the mistakes and the successes of Log Cabin and other organizations, to make sure we had a solid strategy in place from the get-go.

One of the things that Log Cabin had always been criticized for was being a liberal Republican organization. Honestly, it wasn't that the members were liberal; it's just that they only focused their advocacy work on the traditionally liberal policies surrounding gay rights. They never really demonstrated their

common ground with the grassroots conservatives in the conservative movement. One notable exception was an effort that
Chris led in support of President Bush's Social Security reform
proposal in 2005. They did that to try to demonstrate loyalty
to the team after they had publicly denounced Bush and with-
held their endorse of Bush's 2004 reelection campaign because
of his support for the Federal Marriage Amendment and anti-
gay campaign strategy. Log Cabin also always seemed only to
court moderate Republicans and gay liberals in their alliances.
Chris and I both had pitched ideas to Log Cabin leaders over
the years that would have targeted more conservative audiences,
but those ideas were always shot down. Now we could do all
those things we always wanted to do to demonstrate our common ground with grassroots conservatives.

Another thing we wanted to do differently from what we had
done at Log Cabin was that we wanted to include straight conservatives in our organization, because pro-gay straight conservatives didn't have an organization representing them either. We
also wanted straight people involved because we wanted them to
show other straight conservatives that it's okay to show support
for gay and lesbian conservatives, that gays weren't the enemy.
That message was more effective coming from them than from
us. That was key to our efforts to show that gays are just like
everyone else; we are all on this team together. We hoped that it
would help to broaden our fund-raising base, too.

Conventional wisdom on the right and the left was that the
gays were part of the coalition of the left. Too often conservatives viewed gays as the political enemy. We knew that was a
false narrative because there were lots of conservative gays like
us. The core of our strategy was to erase that "us versus them"
mindset and to demonstrate our common ground with other

conservatives. We wanted to fundamentally change the politics regarding gay people and the issues that affect them. The truth was that showing gays on the side of grassroots conservatives would be a win-win for everyone—the gays *and* the conservative movement. The smart folks on both sides understood that, so of course that would bring attacks from the folks who benefited from the status quo. Both the anti-gay organizations on the right and the pro-gay organizations on the left benefited financially from a two-sides status quo. If they were seen as integral parts of their side's coalition, that strengthened their case when fund-raising. Many of them attacked our efforts because they wouldn't have benefited from the political sea change we sought to cause. We wanted a fundamental shift in the politics regarding gay people and the issues that affect them. That was the ultimate goal of the organization that we would call GOProud. (It's pronounced "go-proud.")

The end result of our efforts to build a national organization representing gay and straight conservatives would be beneficial for both the conservative movement and the gay-rights movement. The conservative movement would benefit by being viewed as culturally modern and inclusive. The gay rights movement would win because the opposition to homosexuality and gays among conservatives would first be muted and then, eventually, dissolve.

We advanced our mission by showing how conservative policies that benefit everyone are good for gay people, too. We supported policy positions such as Social Security reform that included private inheritable accounts, abolishing the estate tax, tax reform including the Fair Tax, and free-market-based proposals. Reforms that treated everyone the same were always at the top of our agenda. That was especially true before civil marriage was legal for gay people. There are over a thousand legal benefits that married couples have that weren't available to gay couples then. We also said that protecting Second Amendment rights is important to gays to prevent their becoming victims of violent crimes, and we were advocates for a strong, engaged foreign policy that took a hard line against human-rights abuses, including against gays, around the world.

Of course, we supported the repeal of both the anti-gay Defense of Marriage Act (DOMA) and the law that banned gays from serving in the military, commonly known as Don't Ask, Don't Tell. We limited the scope of our work to federal issues only, in part because that's all we had the capacity to work on, but also because that kept us from taking an official position on marriage beyond repeal of the federal law DOMA. We didn't want to be known as just a "gay-marriage group." That would distract from our efforts to demonstrate our common ground with conservatives who might not support marriage equality. That was something we would often point to when our attackers on the right would call us "nothing but a gay-marriage organization." We would say that we didn't take a position on that except that the federal government should recognize same-sex marriages performed in the states where it was legal. We never officially expressed our opinion on whether state bans on civil marriage for gay couples violated the US Constitution. (They did.) Of course, Chris and another board member, Jessica Lee, married their partners almost as soon as marriage was legal in the District of Columbia, but it wasn't officially part of our scope of work when we started.

Everyone who works in politics knows that sometimes, when you want to advance your position, you have to pick a fight. GOProud's first fight would be within our own family, with the straggling members of Log Cabin, who were trying to keep that organization alive and saw us as a threat. Once we decided to move forward with our new group and decided on the name, we started to plan our launch. We made some calls to get a few commitments for funding that totaled approximately $30,000, and we recruited our friend Bruce Carroll to join the board as our treasurer. It was getting close to tax day, so we decided to launch on April 15th for the symbolic statement that gays hate taxes too.

The ironic thing about launching on that date was that what was left of the Log Cabin group was planning a gathering in DC then too. They didn't have any staff, but were working hard to show that they still existed. We planned our announcement on Wednesday and their gathering was on Friday and Saturday of that week. Fireworks erupted early that week when our launch was featured in Bill McGurn's *Wall Street Journal* column on that Tuesday. The Log Cabin folks clearly saw GOProud as competition to them. They went into full-scale attack behind the scenes, calling reporters and potential donors, trying to discredit us.

Before Log Cabin had closed their office earlier that year, they had interviewed both Chris and me as potential executive directors to lead and try to revive the organization. They ultimately decided to go without full-time staff. When we launched GOProud, their attack on us was that we were bitter and had sour grapes because neither of us had been chosen to lead that group. Their argument didn't hold water because they were barely an organization at that point. In the end, they were successful in getting some of the financial pledges made to us canceled, but the truth was that their pettiness just further diminished their already weakened brand.

We launched GOProud and set out to build a solid conservative brand for it. Our next fight was more fun, and it helped to put us clearly on the side of other conservatives: We became the lead group advocating for a pro-gun amendment to the proposed federal hate-crimes legislation. The hate-crimes bill had passed both the House and the Senate at different times in previous years, but had never made it to the president's desk before. This time it was sure to pass and become law. We demonstrated that we were team players with conservatives by being out front on the Republican concealed carry reciprocity amendment. The gays on the left attacked us, claiming that the gun amendment was a poison pill that would kill the hate-crimes legislation. We didn't mind the attacks because demonstrating that we were on the conservative team meant that the other team had to attack us to show that we weren't on their team.

To be honest, attaching the pro-gun amendment to the hate-crimes bill was a brilliant idea that should have created a bill that everyone in the Senate could support. The liberal senators couldn't vote against the gay bill and the conservative ones couldn't vote against the gun bill. That didn't happen, because the Democrats found enough opposition to the gun amendment to keep it from being attached to the bill, but we were encouraged by the whole experience because we knew that the premise of our strategy was a good one.

We showed that we were team players, and our team reciprocated. Kansas Senator Sam Brownback had attempted to offer an amendment to the hate-crimes bill that would have banned same-sex marriage in the District of Columbia, ending a debate that was raging in DC at the time. The GOP leadership killed his amendment because they decided to get behind the gun proposal, and one Senate aide said to us, "they didn't want to do that to you guys, since you have carried the water on the concealed carry amendment." YES! Being a team player could be a two-way street. We were proving it.

So with very little money in the bank, and just Chris and me with our laptops, we set out to show the world that not all gays are liberals and not all conservatives are anti-gay homophobes. I didn't have any other choice. I didn't have a job, and there are just times in life when you come to understand that you are meant to do something important, so you just have to find a way to do it.

That first year was tough. We had some great successes but also a lot of setbacks. It was difficult for me financially. I sold most of my furniture, and moved out of my apartment into a group house in a marginal neighborhood. There wasn't always a paycheck every month in those early days. It was truly a labor of love. I admit that I did have some resentment toward Chris because he had several consulting clients and a partner with a full-time job to sustain him in those lean times. I was on my own with no choice but to make GOProud work.

We were growing the brand, and it helped that another political movement was growing then too—the Tea Party. The original message of the Tea Party was about rolling back the size and scope of government. It was about getting control of the spending in Washington and devolving power from the DC establishment to the people in the states. That was a message that resonated with our folks. Most gay people have always generally wanted limited government, and of course in a system that uses the tax code and other forces of government to pick winners and losers, gays were more often than not the losers. Challenging the status quo in government and politics was a natural fit for us.

The biggest specific issue galvanizing the movement was the opposition to President Obama's healthcare reform proposal. As free-market conservatives, we preferred reforms that empowered individuals to make decisions in their healthcare by allowing everyone to go on the open market to find insurance plans that met their individual needs. Government-based or employer-based healthcare systems put that power in others' hands. There are unique healthcare-related situations that apply to gays, and we wanted them to make the decisions that met their needs. For instance, we didn't want the government or employer to be the ones determining if a same-sex couple could have a family insurance policy that covered everyone in their household. We enthusiastically supported the Tea Party effort to oppose Obama's government-based healthcare proposal.

We made friends in the Tea Party movement and joined the cause. We were the Tea Party gays! It was a great opportunity to challenge conventional wisdom and show that we were team players with conservatives at the same time!

I'll never forget marching in the Taxpayers March on Washington on September 12, 2009. There were tens of thousands marching down Pennsylvania Avenue to the Capitol. I kept seeing gays, lots of gays, marching in the crowd. They were happy to see me, the new leader of the gay right, marching with them in what would be seen later as the official launch of the Tea Party as a national movement. The Tea Party was where all the energy and influence was on the right then, and with their limited-government message, Tea Party activists were the perfect audience for our message too.

By the fall of that year, GOProud was really on the edge financially. It was questionable how much longer we could go on. I certainly didn't know how much longer I could personally survive. We were able to scrape up enough money to sign on as a cosponsor of the Conservative Political Action Conference, commonly known as CPAC. It took nearly everything we had to pay the $3,500 sponsorship fee, but we did it because it was important. Nothing else we could have done that year would demonstrate that we were part of the team as effectively as being a cosponsor of CPAC. GOProud was one of dozens of sponsoring organizations, most of them well known in the conservative movement.

As soon as our check arrived at the offices of the American Conservative Union (ACU), the organization that produces CPAC, the opposition mobilized against our inclusion in the conference. One of the ACU's board members, Washington lawyer Cleta Mitchell, had it out for us from the beginning, and it was personal for her. You see, Cleta's first husband had left her for a man, and she never got over it. Cleta did not want gays at CPAC. She began to work behind the scenes with others to organize opposition to GOProud's participation. Several prominent social conservatives began to raise objection to GOProud's sponsorship in the press.

That was one of the coldest winters I can remember, and it was also the winter of the biggest blizzard Washington had ever seen. The CPAC sponsorship controversy was raging in the press, with several organizations threatening to boycott the event, and I was sitting at home watching the blizzard and suffering from the dreaded swine flu. That's right. I had a 105-degree fever, no health insurance, no money, no food, and no medicine. I was at the end of my rope. I didn't know what I was going to do. I thought that if I could make it to CPAC, then I could decide if I was going to continue on this GOProud journey or not.

One of the cool things about being a sponsor of CPAC was that we got to participate in the conference planning meetings with the other sponsors. That's where the organizers go over the logistics and hear input about programming and suggestions for speakers. I had caught the swine flu a few weeks before CPAC. I had recovered from it enough to make it to the final CPAC planning meeting, but I looked horrible. I had lost a ton of weight and still had a bit of cough and runny nose, but, given the situation with the opposition, I couldn't skip it. I'm sure that many of the conservative leaders in the room thought I was suffering from AIDS, since of course I was the gay.

I remember David Keene, the ACU chairman, made a point of coming over and shaking my hand. David is a giant in the conservative movement. He's been around since the 1960s and wields considerable influence. He knows that gays have always been a part of the movement and he was committed to making sure that GOProud had an official seat at the table. He was responsible for beating back the opposition and allowing GOProud to be a cosponsor. That day at the planning meeting was the first time I had the opportunity to meet him in person, but it wouldn't be the last. Unbeknownst to both of us, the controversy around our sponsorship of CPAC 2010 was just the tip of the iceberg when it came to opposition to GOProud from the right. David would prove to be a key ally over the next couple years when things would heat up considerably.

We made it to CPAC. I was feeling better physically, but I was nervous as hell about what we might encounter there. There had been so much press about us leading up to the event that everyone there knew who we were. Chris and I had come up with a little bit of a gimmick to try to get some attention, and show that we were true conservatives. "Draft Cheney 2012" was our CPAC 2010 campaign. We had rolls of stickers and a few signs. It was really cool, especially when former Vice President Dick Cheney stepped onto the stage as a surprise speaker. A CNN producer who interviewed us that morning tipped us off, so we made sure to have our volunteers at the door of the ballroom distributing our stickers to everyone there. They were a real hit with the crowd and got us a little positive press attention. I later gave the leftover stickers to Vice President Cheney's daughter Mary for the Cheney grandchildren to play with.

The truth is, even though some people stirred controversy in the press, most of the anti-gay right didn't see us as a real threat. They saw us as a small group, with no money and no influence. At CPAC, we had a sad little booth with a few dedicated volunteers, but we didn't appear to be a well-funded operation with a lot of people. The rule in politics is to shoot up, not down, so the biggest anti-gay names mostly ignored us once the conference started. The anti-gay organization National Organization for Marriage did fire one shot at us during the conference via press release, warning GOProud that they would work to defeat any pro-gay-marriage candidates we supported in Republican primary elections. There really wasn't significant controversy until Ryan Sorba, a young conservative activist, used his five minutes on the main stage of the conference to denounce the ACU for allowing us to sponsor the event. The crowd erupted with boos. They booed him off the stage. The grassroots conservatives in the crowd clearly stood with GOProud!

I didn't know what had happened on the stage, but soon after Sorba was booed, I got a couple of emails on my smartphone from our online donations service letting me know that people had made donations. We went into CPAC with about $400 in the bank. I didn't think we would stay open much longer. By the end of that day, after news that Sorba was booed by the audience began to circulate, we had a couple of thousand dollars in small contributions from people across the country who saw the impact we were having on the conservative movement, and they wanted to support us.

The demonstration of support from the crowd boosted our confidence and our profile that day. We were trying to clean up our booth in the vendor area, but we were swamped with reporters getting our take on what had happened in the conventional hall that day. One of those reporters was John Avlon with The Daily Beast. John said that we should meet his wife, then FOX News commentator Margaret Hoover, who was also a prominent conservative advocate for legal civil marriage for gay couples. I knew of Margaret and definitely wanted to meet her.

A few weeks later, Chris and I had lunch with Margaret in Washington. Margaret also worked for Paul Singer, a hedge fund manager and well-known Republican megadonor. Paul also gave heavily to gay rights causes because his son is gay. Margaret wanted to hear more about our strategy to create an atmosphere on the right where gays were a real part of the coalition and straight conservatives could voice support on issues affecting gay people without fear of retribution from the anti-gay right. Margaret got it. She loved it and thought Paul would be interested in GOProud too. She understood how support of GOProud would benefit both of Paul's biggest priorities: his support of gay rights and Republican candidates.

Paul Singer wasn't the only major donor whose radar we were on. I had recently been introduced, through a mutual friend via email, to Peter Thiel. Peter was the openly gay, libertarian technology entrepreneur and founder of PayPal. Peter agreed to meet with Chris and me in his New York apartment.

We had some great new prospects, but we still didn't have very much money. It took almost everything we had in the bank that day to get Amtrak tickets to New York for Chris and me. We had to get up at 4 a.m. to catch a train to make it to our 10 a.m. meeting with Peter, because we didn't have the money for a hotel room. That seemed like the longest train ride ever. A lot was riding on that meeting, and I was nervous.

Peter is from Silicon Valley, where young billionaires wear jeans and hoodies to work. We knew not to wear ties, but we did wear suits—just no ties. I was so poor that one of my shoes had a hole in the bottom of it.

When we arrived at Peter's house I felt a little out of place. He lived in a huge penthouse apartment on the fifty-fourth floor of the Bloomberg Building on 58th Street in Manhattan. When we got to the building, I was struck at how many staff people the building had. Doormen and security guards with earpieces made sure we got to the correct elevator and whisked up to the top floor. We were greeted at the door by Peter's chef, who showed us into the expansive living room and offered us something to drink. The apartment had all-glass walls that gave you the feeling of floating high up in the atmosphere.

The furniture was very contemporary and sat low to the ground. It was kind of like Mame Dennis's apartment in the Rosalind Russell movie version of *Auntie Mame* after she had it redesigned by the Danish designer Yul Ulu! Chris was on the couch and I sat in a chair that was so low I felt like I was sitting on the ground. Peter came in and sat on an ottoman across from me. He was perched up much higher than me. I thought this must be part of his body language strategy, so that he had the upper hand in meetings. Of course he did anyway. He was the one with the money.

I just remember thinking to myself, *Jimmy, don't cross your legs. He might see the hole in your shoe!* The chef came around with coffee every few minutes, so punctual that our cups were never empty and it never got cold. His timing was so perfect that I was convinced he had hidden cameras so that he could see when we needed a refill.

As predicted, Peter was a super-casual guy, in jeans and a polo shirt, but he was serious and all business in our meeting. He liked what we were doing with GOProud. He too was a limited-government gay who felt that there was a need for our voice on the national political landscape. The moment came to ask for the money and I did it. I told him that we needed to raise $250k in the next couple of months to really get our group going and we wanted him to be a part of the group of donors who made that possible. He said that he didn't want to do the whole thing but he would do something. He'd do at least $50k, but wanted to think about it. I was to follow up with him in a couple of weeks. YES! He said yes!

Chris and I got into the elevator to leave and he whispered to me not to react in the elevator because we were probably on camera. We got outside and Chris said, "That went really well!"

"Peter's really cute," I replied.

Chris hit me in the arm and said, "This is business!"

We were ecstatic and we knew that we were on a roll and that we were actually going to make something of GOProud.

A few weeks later I called Peter to follow up on our conversation. He asked what we had been up to since our meeting in New York, and I told him that we were planning a fund-raising event in New York City later in the summer featuring bestselling author and conservative commentator Ann Coulter. I told him that we had had our friend Americans for Tax Reform president Grover Norquist reach out to Ann to ask her if she would headline a fund-raiser for us. Ann replied to his email, "Of course I'll do it. I'm the Judy Garland of the right wing!" Peter thought that her response was hysterically funny. He told me that he had met her and thought she was very smart. He suggested that we should have the event at his place. What I would learn later was that Ann and Peter were actually good friends, very good friends. (He didn't tell me that because he likes to keep things close to the vest.) That was a stroke of luck. Peter would host our event featuring his friend Ann Coulter! Peter also committed to giving us $100k. That was by far the largest contribution we had received up to that point.

It took us a few weeks to work out the details, but we knew that when the news broke of right-wing provocateur Ann Coulter headlining a gay event at famous gay billionaire Peter Thiel's home, folks on the left and the right would lose their shit! The left was outraged that we would want a hardcore conservative like Ann at our event, and the anti-gay right knew that we would be a real threat now that we had well-known solid conservatives like Grover and Ann and big money donors like Peter supporting us.

We decided to call the event "Homocon," which was a term that the gay left used in a derogatory way to describe gay conservatives. We embraced it and owned it. It was edgy and outside the box, just like we were. Calling the event something like "An Evening with Ann Coulter" would have been douchey and conventional. That wasn't us. The announcement of our Homocon event made headlines, and it sold out in short order.

It was a busy summer. Before we could do the Homocon event in New York, we had another reception to do in California, and it was also controversial. In 2008, Doug Manchester, the owner of the Manchester Grand Hyatt Resort in San Diego and a major GOP donor, gave money to help launch the campaign to pass California's anti-gay marriage amendment, Proposition 8. That donation sparked a boycott, led by the liberal gay organizations, of Manchester's hotel properties.

By 2010, Manchester had come to regret his past support for Proposition 8, and in fact changed his position on it. He realized the mistake he had made, I think, in part, because nearly a third of the employees at the Manchester Hyatt were gay! Mr. Manchester was seeking to make amends with the gay community, promising grants and the use of the hotel to LGBT organizations. Most organizations balked. We didn't. We accepted a contribution and planned a reception at the hotel.

Our board member Jessica Lee and a couple of volunteers flew out from Washington with Chris and me. We arrived in San Diego where we were greeted by a police detective warning us that there had been threats made against us by liberal gays and to also expect protests of our event. Sure enough, the next day at our event, there were protestors. There was a line of policemen and police cars surrounding the hotel protecting us, but one of the protestors did make it into our event. They were quickly escorted out by hotel security.

I couldn't understand why there were protests. Didn't the gays want people who once opposed civil marriage for gay couples to change their minds? Wasn't that the point? Manchester had apologized for his past support of Proposition 8, but that wasn't enough for the gay left—they wanted retribution. I have never thought that seeking retribution for past actions based on today's standards and norms was productive. That's especially true while cultural evolution is still happening. We had moved public opinion significantly since 2008, but in 2010 we hadn't reached the tipping point on marriage yet.

Now, leading up to our event in New York, I was starting to get worried that there would be protests of our event with Ann too. Ann didn't support marriage equality and the gay left *hated* her. The gay left would never accept anything short of support for "full equality," as they put it. They didn't understand that the grassroots of the conservative movement just wasn't there, but we could do a lot to diminish animosity toward gays by having people like Ann publicly embrace us and tell her audience that "just because you are born gay, doesn't mean that you are born liberal." What the gay left activists didn't understand was that when Ann said to her audience that people were born gay, it was a much more powerful statement than any gay person could deliver to that audience. They needed to hear that from her.

We'd hoped that the gay community would see that conservatives like Ann, who weren't where we would like them to be on marriage, weren't necessarily anti-gay homophobes. In fact, in Ann's case, she's basically a fag hag! (That's a slang term for a single straight woman who has mostly gay male friends.)

A couple of days before our party in New York, Paul Singer was hosting a fund-raiser at the Mandarin Oriental Hotel in Manhattan in support of the lawsuit challenging Proposition 8 in federal court. (That suit would eventually end up with a victory when US Supreme Court struck down Prop 8, legalizing gay marriage in California.) By then, Singer had given GOProud money, and Peter was a cohost of the Singer event, so Chris and I definitely went to it. Before the Singer reception we met with *New York Times* reporter Laura Holson in the lounge of the hotel. She was doing a big story about Ann and our event for the *Times's* Sunday Style section.

The lounge at the Mandarin is on a high floor overlooking Columbus Circle, Central Park, and all of New York City. We sat with Holson at a table in front of the windows. For a moment, I just sat there thinking about where we were six months ago—dead broke and about to go out of business. Now, here we sat in this fancy place with an amazing view, with two billionaire donors and a *New York Times* Sunday Style feature story! I looked out over the city, and literally felt on top of the world. Some of the gays going to the Singer reception saw us doing the interview, and I could tell that they were talking about us as they walked past. They knew that we were doing amazing work, and getting a lot of attention for it. Their resentment toward us was palpable. Chris said something funny that I'll never forget. He looked at me and said, "This is what it feels like to be the prettiest girls in school." I loved that! That's exactly what it felt like.

Later that night I had dinner with Peter at the Standard Grill in New York's trendy meatpacking district. It was similar to many other experiences I had while running a national gay organization, when I wasn't exactly sure if I was on a fund-raising dinner or a date. Peter and I definitely had a connection. It's not often in the gay world when you come across an attractive and smart guy who you sync with politically. There was chemistry, but in the end, nothing ended up happening on the romantic front with us. It just wasn't a match but I was grateful for his support.

I was excited for our Homocon party and the message that it would send to the right and the left, but I was still worried about potential protests that could disrupt the event. As luck would have it, Peter moved into a new apartment a month or so before our event there, so the location of his residence wasn't widely known and the protestors didn't know where to protest our event! He had downsized to a gorgeous, but smaller, place on Union Square. We had room for about 150 people, and we had sold out weeks before. There were no protestors outside.

Peter's staff did an amazing job putting the party together. The waiters and bartenders were gorgeous models, a hip DJ played cool music, the food was delicious—the champagne was Dom Perignon, for crying out loud—it was just that kind of night! The crowd included some famous FOX News personalities and other well-known conservatives, and the whole beautiful scene created exactly what we wanted to show the world—conservatives and gays can be on the same team. It also showed the conservative movement as a cool, modern, and culturally connected political movement. The best part of the whole thing was that it was documented in the *New York Times* with photos!

4

WINNING TEAM

By the fall of 2010, GOProud was flush with cash and on a roll. I found a little English basement office for us to rent on Capitol Hill. I was still living in the crappy house with roommates, so I couldn't really work from home, and we were growing so fast that we needed office space. We were getting more and more engaged in the midterm elections, and we were endorsing candidates. This was the Tea Party election and the Republicans were poised to win a majority in the US House, and we wanted to make sure that gays were contributing members of the winning team on Election Day.

We certainly had many disagreements in all of the years we worked together, but one thing I know for sure: Chris and I were one of the most creative duos in politics. We were the ones who had Ann Coulter headline a gay event, remember. So with the midterm elections approaching, we put our heads together to come up with a creative way to help elect a Republican majority in Washington, and to show that the gays were on the team.

One thing that many of the smart people on the right, including Chris and me, had always said was that Republicans need to do better at recognizing and embracing the power of culture, including pop culture, in politics. For too many Republicans, politics was all about policy, data, and analytics. We got it, though. After all, we were the gays.

Chris and I usually talked on the phone every morning about 7:30 a.m. while I was on the way to the office. He did not always work from the office, but called every morning so we could come up with our plan and scheme for the day. One day in September 2010, we had a stroke of genius while on our morning call. He and I had had many ideas, but usually it was one of us coming up with the idea, then both of us fleshing it out. This time, our idea was 100 percent collaborative in its inception. I think it turned out to be the best idea ever for a political ad.

We came up with an innovative ad that would target gays and female voters by integrating pop culture into a political message. We would connect on a personal level by putting the argument in the context of something those voters were familiar with, like their favorite television show. Our ad was a play on our favorite show, *The Real Housewives*. We produced "The Real Democrats of Washington, DC"! It was a spoof of the *Real Housewives* opening credits featuring prominent Democrats. The narrator, who we hired because his voice was similar to *Real Housewives* creator Andy Cohen's, began with, "If you thought the housewives were dysfunctional, wait until you meet the Real Democrats of Washington, DC"! The ad closed with "Under Democrats, reality bites!" It was just awesome.

We aired the ad in four states with close races, including in Massachusetts against openly gay Congressman Barney Frank. He wasn't pleased. The ad called him "catty"! The ad ran for ten days before the election, including during *The Real Housewives* show on Bravo and during the *Project Runway* season finale on Lifetime. We knew we'd reach lots of gays and straight women with ad buys on those networks. It turned out that they weren't the only ones watching.

The night before the election, my phone started blowing up with text messages and phone calls alerting me to the fact that the FOX News Channel's *Hannity Show* was featuring our ad in a show about the political ads of the 2010 midterms. Pollster Frank Luntz had convened a focus group of voters in Cleveland to dial test ads from across the country to see how real voters reacted to them. In the last segment of the show, Luntz came on and looked at the camera and said to the host Sean Hannity, "Sean, we tested a lot of ads today, but there was one ad that tested better than any other. . . ." He looked at the focus group and asked, "Wasn't it one of the best ads you've ever seen?" It was our ad! Our ad tested better with real voters than any other ad in the country that year! The best part was that the FOX News audience of over three million conservatives that night saw that GOProud, the gay group, was running a great ad against Democrats. The message to them was that the gays are on your team. We could never have bought that kind of publicity for the work we were doing, and we could never have paid to deliver that message to that FOX News audience.

There was one incident during that election cycle that was a disappointing reminder of the reality of what we were up against. One of our grassroots members in Missouri, Joe Bowmaster, was a prominent Tea Party activist there. Joe organized a rally in his hometown a few days before the election. The rally was going to feature a speech by the local candidate for the US House, Vicky Hartzler, who was in a tight race challenging the longtime incumbent Democratic Congressman Ike Skelton.

Joe was proud of being a part of GOProud, and he asked me if he could list GOProud as one of many organizations sponsoring the Tea Party rally he was organizing. We didn't give him any money or anything for our "sponsorship." Joe just wanted to list as many organizations as possible on the sponsorship list to show a broad-based, inclusive coalition. I thought it was great!

Vicky Hartzler was a state legislator who had made her name as the lead anti-gay crusader in the Missouri House of Representatives. She is a real piece of work. A day or two before the rally, her campaign staff informed Joe that Vicky would be "too embarrassed" to appear at an event that had a gay group as a sponsor. I was shocked. Joe was hurt and humiliated. He didn't want to have to tell the other Tea Party activists in Missouri that their candidate would not appear at their event because she was too embarrassed to participate in an event sponsored by people like him.

I reached out to the campaign and tried to convince them that they were making a mistake. I told her staff that this election was about unity and they were stomping on that message, not to mention the bigotry of it all. I said that I could make this incident into a big national news story if I wanted to. They knew that, but they also knew that a fight with the gays wouldn't hurt their candidate in that rural Missouri district. I also repeatedly asked to speak with Hartzler herself, but was denied. I guess she couldn't bring herself to even get on the phone with a gay person.

I knew that the national media would love to run with a story that would show that a Tea Party candidate was an anti-gay bigot. That's what they wanted the country to think about the Tea Party. MSNBC, especially, would have me on every hour from then until the election if I wanted that. It would be a huge national story, on the weekend before the election, that would damage the Republican brand and actually politically hurt other Republican candidates across the country more than it would hurt Hartzler.

No matter how mad I was, I knew that I couldn't go nuclear on Hartzler in the media. Our whole strategy was to be team players. I told Joe to remove GOProud's name from the sponsorship list. The rally went on with Hartzler and without GOProud. Hartzler went on to win her election to Congress. Then I called Mike Bober, the coalitions director at the National Republican Congressional Committee, the party entity that oversees US House candidates. I made sure that he knew that GOProud was being a team player by not blowing up a national story about GOP bigotry on the weekend before the election. It goes without saying that Hartzler has been one of the leading anti-gay voices in Congress ever since.

Republicans did take control of the House in the Tea Party election of 2010. According to CNN's exit polls, 32 percent of gay voters voted for the GOP candidate for Congress in their districts. That's right, nearly a third of gays voted Republican that year. The gay vote accounted for more GOP votes than blacks, Asians, Jews, and many, many other demographic groups. It affirmed that Republicans could win votes when their message was about rolling back the size and scope of government and not about cultural issues like gay marriage. They also won when they showed that their team was a broad, diverse coalition that included everyone.

After the election, there was a contentious lame duck session of Congress, and we were in the middle of it. Before the election, the Democrats had staged some votes for repeal of Don't Ask, Don't Tell for political purposes, but now was the time to actually move the bill to repeal the discriminatory law. Everyone knew that the new GOP majority in the House wouldn't bring the bill up for a vote, so it had to pass the House and Senate in a matter of a couple of weeks.

On November 16, ahead of the lame duck session, Chris and I had a secret meeting in the West Wing of the White House. I had met the deputy director of public liaison and LGBT outreach director, Brian Bond, when I first moved to Washington, when he worked at the Democratic National Committee, and he and I had a good working relationship. Brian arranged a meeting with his boss, Tina Tchen, and a few other senior people to see if we could help in the effort to pass the DADT repeal bill.

It was an interesting day at the White House. Chris and I arrived in the West Wing just as the president was presenting the Medal of Honor to Army Sergeant Salvatore Giunta, the first living service member from the Iraq or Afghanistan wars to receive it. It was ironic that we were there to meet about military policy, and it was a stroke of luck because many of the key players were at the White House for the medal ceremony. During our meeting, the Pentagon liaison who was meeting with us got up and left to walk down the hall to the Oval Office to join the president, the chairman of the joint chiefs of staff, and the secretary of defense.

When we sat down, Tchen said something like, "You all have employed a very smart strategy in your work. All the other gay groups have done all they can do to help pass this bill; how can you use your conservative credibility to help us?" We supplied some important intelligence from some of our behind-the-scenes work that nobody else knew. We told them about a couple of members of the Senate who were on the fence, and what their key pressure points were. It was clear to me in that meeting that the White House didn't really have good relationships with very many of the president's former colleagues in the Senate, even some of the more moderate ones.

I was in Louisiana on the day of the vote to repeal DADT in the Senate. I remember being in the car with a donor from Texas, Jay Bowen, while I was on the phone with Brian asking him to get the president to personally call a conservative senator who was on the fence. The vote was imminent and we had heard from gay Republican staffers that this senator was undecided. I was hopeful that a call from the president would tip the balance. I don't know if that call actually happened or not. That particular senator ended up voting no. I suspected that once they had enough votes to pass the bill, they stopped trying to get more Republicans to support it. The White House didn't want it to look too bipartisan because they would need their gay constituency mobilized for the president's reelection, and it would help if he and the Democrats got all the credit for DADT repeal.

I was just glad that the tens of thousands of gay and lesbian American patriots, who risk their lives for all of us, could now legally live their lives openly and honestly without having to keep part of who they were in the closet. I was proud of the role we played in making that happen, no matter who got the credit.

5

HAND-TO-HAND COMBAT

Now we were full-fledged conservative celebrities, and more importantly, we had big names—bigger than we'd ever be—who were squarely in our corner. We were no longer just two guys and our laptops, with a few pamphlets at CPAC. We were the real deal now, and the target on our backs was bigger than ever.

We were making real progress in changing the anti-gay atmosphere on the right, and the crazies knew it. They redoubled their efforts to keep us out of the next CPAC. Their effort was intense. Again, the ringleader was Washington lawyer and ACU board member Cleta Mitchell. Cleta is a typical Washington behind-the-scenes operator, the type that works in the shadows and only takes credit for their dirty work at cocktail parties, not in the media. Cleta and her band of bigots had their act together this time and their knives were out for us.

The effort to organize a full-scale boycott was in full swing by the fall of 2010 and it appeared to be picking up steam. Just like the previous year, very few of the boycotters had actually been a part of CPAC in recent years, but by early December there were reports that the giant conservative think tank, The Heritage Foundation, was considering joining the boycott. Cleta's buddy

Becky Dunlop was in charge of that decision at Heritage. So the outcome was already likely determined.

ACU Chairman David Keene understood that this year would be different and engaged with us early in the fall. He and Chris worked together to show the crazies that we belonged at CPAC. Chris met with several groups, including Focus on the Family, in an effort to convince them that we were true conservatives, and we made even more of an effort to highlight our conservative credentials. I even gave a speech to George Washington University's pro-life group about why all gay people should be pro-life. Over and over again we reminded people that we didn't have a position on marriage, except that DOMA should be repealed and the federal government should stay out of marriage because the Constitution left marriage and family law to the states.

At Keene's request, I kept my distance from the planning meetings that all the other cosponsors attended, and we just generally kept our heads down. It was hard to do because it was starting to blow up in the press, but the behind-the-scenes drama was really something, too. It was truly humiliating to agree to be treated differently from all the other sponsors, simply because we were gay, but I thought it could result in a good thing in the long run.

In the end, our attempt to show our conservative bona fides was a futile effort because many on the right just don't believe that gay people are capable of holding conservative views. By December, we were in full-scale war. Cleta had her minions (a.k.a. clients) doing much of her dirty work for her. She was urging speakers to boycott the conference and was successful in getting her clients, then Senator Jim DeMint and Congressman Jim Jordan, to publicly announce that they were boycotting CPAC because of

GOProud. Former Senator Jim Talent, at Cleta's behest, called presumed presidential candidate Mitt Romney to urge him to boycott. (Romney didn't comply with that request.)

Former Labor Secretary and Heritage Foundation Distinguished Fellow Elaine Chao had asked Singer for a significant donation to fund her work at Heritage. Once the Heritage CPAC boycott was finally announced after a month or so of speculation, Singer sent a barn burner of a letter to Chao and Heritage's president Ed Feulner letting them know exactly why he was declining their request for funding. I was told that Chao later privately expressed concern to Singer about the extremist agenda that Heritage was promoting. Chao remained at Heritage, though, so she must not have been that concerned about the direction of the organization. Since then, Jim DeMint has assumed Feulner's job as Heritage's president and the agenda has become even more extreme.

Keeping our heads down was not an option as CPAC drew nearer. There was just too much swirling in the press for that. We were in full-scale war. It was all our little office could do to keep up with it. It was like Grand Central Station around there. We had reporters and photographers in and out of the office constantly in the weeks leading up to CPAC.

One day that January, I was skimming the news stories online at the end of the day. Then I picked up the phone and called Chris. I screamed at him, "Look at the *NY Times* website *right now!*" Their photographer had been to our office a few days before and there it was: the big picture on the main page of their website was a photo of Chris and me. A long story about us and the CPAC controversy appeared in the print edition of the paper the next morning.

I remember saying to Chris, "This is what winning looks like." I had always known in my heart that we were right and that we would win. I just never really knew for sure how we would get there. This was it. We were winning and there was no going back. It appeared that we were finally beating the anti-gay bigots and the conservative movement was turning pro-gay, and it was all because of us.

A few weeks before CPAC, conservative media mogul Andrew Breitbart said during a radio interview that he supported GOProud's sponsorship of CPAC and would host a big gay '80s dance party during CPAC to demonstrate his support of a conservative movement that included gays. I spoke with him on the phone the next day. He agreed to join our advisory council, and we set out to plan the Big Party. We named it Big Party because most of the Breitbart Company news and commentary websites began with "Big," such as BigGovernment. com. Andrew and I began what would be a sometimes rocky but mutually beneficial relationship.

Andrew was a giant in the conservative universe. He was a bomb-thrower, and he had a loyal and devoted following. His small, but growing company was essentially the mouthpiece of the Tea Party movement. Many grassroots activists took their cues from Andrew and the Breitbart Company staff. We were ecstatic to have them publicly on our side.

For Andrew, more than almost anyone I've ever met in politics, except for maybe FOX News Channel founder Roger Ailes, it was all about "us versus them." He didn't always take positions on specific policy issues. He was all about waging war with the left, period. He was the perfect messenger for our strategy of removing the "us versus them" narrative between conservatives and gays. The gays are on our team now! Now come on, let's continue to fight the left! We were also beneficial to Andrew's effort to grow the conservative movement. He had a keen sense of cultural evolution and he knew that a movement that was seen as anti-gay would be out of touch. He used GOProud to demonstrate that conservatives were modern and in touch with real life in America.

The media firestorm was raging. In addition to the *New York Times* article, Chris and I were both all over the news, including television, radio, and print. We were depicted in a cartoon on the cover of the LGBT magazine *Metro Weekly* that came out the day CPAC started. The *Metro Weekly* interview with both of us was done a couple of weeks before CPAC in our office with the prominent gay reporter Chris Geidner.

In the *Metro Weekly* story, Chris and I made an impassioned defense of the conservative movement. We said that conservative policies benefit everyone, including gay people. We said that very few conservatives actually fit the liberal narrative that "all conservatives are anti-gay homophobes," and we said that the movement is inclusive of gays. We did acknowledge that there were some in the movement who just didn't like gay people, but that they were in the minority. Chris used Cleta as an example of one of those people. He referred to her as a "nasty bigot."

We had done a pretty good job in the months leading up to CPAC of letting our friends do most of the attacking in the press. That's usually a good strategy. I remember thinking at the time that we should ask to keep that "nasty bigot" comment out of the story, but I didn't say anything because the media frenzy was at a point where everyone involved was just letting it fly, so why should we hold back? Besides, Chris was right, she is a nasty bigot.

Our little office was buzzing with activity. We had a group of young people whom I called "The Grasshoppers" helping us. They were interns and paid staff working on folding tables and chairs. Singer sent us a check to cover our CPAC expenses and to pay for the Breitbart party. (He also sent the ACU a big check that more than made up for any revenue they might have lost from the sponsorships of the few boycotting organizations.) It was a big change from last year's CPAC when we were just a few volunteers and some pamphlets.

We had a first-class operation at the CPAC hotel, where I rented a large one-bedroom suite. We had volunteers and staff, and all the bells and whistles. Our booth in the vendor area looked amazing, and our Big Party with Andrew Breitbart was the hottest ticket at the conference.

We were a little concerned heading into CPAC that there could be confrontations or even physical attacks on us, but I decided to cut the personal protection details for Chris and me from the budget once the party expenses started to balloon. Personal security was always in the back of my mind that whole week. We had received some threatening emails and a couple of crazy voice messages from anti-gay zealots that caused me to be a little nervous. Our friend Floyd Resnick, a former NYC policeman whom we met when he was Ann's bodyguard at our Homocon event, was running the security for the conference. Floyd assured me that he would take care of anyone who gave his gay friends trouble!

There was a line around the block of activists braving frigid temperatures to be a part of our Big Party. The room projected exactly the message we intended to send to the world. Conservatives are hip, cool, and gay-loving! The band was set up in front of a banner of a rock-n-roll heart with wings, with GOPROUD written on a tattoo-style sash across the heart. There was '80s music played by a DJ who was also projecting '80s music videos and GOProud logos on the walls. Four hundred fifty people crammed into the room to hear our headliner, Grammy-nominated singer and songwriter Sophie B. Hawkins. It was the biggest gay event ever at a conservative conference.

Before Sophie sang, I stepped onto the stage to welcome everyone and thank them for their support. While I was making my remarks, out of the corner of my eye I could see Andrew dart out of the room. I thought, oh damn, where's he going? It's his turn to speak in a minute. Chris said a few words after I spoke, and then introduced Andrew. He wasn't there. In a minute Andrew reemerged to take the stage with former Republican National Committee Chairman Michael Steele, a surprise guest. Andrew had left for a minute to go outside to usher Steele into the party because he was stuck outside standing in the line on the sidewalk waiting to get in!

Andrew made some remarks that included, "We are making conservative history here tonight." He was right. We were making history. The grassroots leaders in the conservative movement publicly embracing the gays! That was unheard of before GOProud. I still can't believe that there are some on the right who don't see the benefit of having gays as a visible part of their coalition. Gay people are part of modern life in America. Public acknowledgment of that would go a long way to help conservatives.

There were a few gay liberals at that event, mostly gay media, who saw firsthand what was happening there. They were stunned. They were stunned for two reasons. First, they saw "the enemy" coalescing with gay people. More importantly, they saw inroads that conservatives could make with an important constituency of the coalition of the left. The message sent to all sides that night was powerful. I was so proud.

I still have people who come up to me to tell me that that was the best party they've ever been to. It really was off-the-hook fun. There were even a couple of straight guys who got into a drunken fight over a girl—now that's a party!

My favorite reported story from that night was by national political reporter Dave Weigel about a conversation that allegedly happened between Michael Steele and Sophie B. Hawkins. Steele told Hawkins that he was glad that she was a conservative. She replied, "I don't call myself a conservative, but I'd fuck Sarah Palin!" She later denied saying that, but I suspect that she actually did because she told me in the dressing room that she would like to be trapped in an igloo during an Alaskan blizzard with Palin! Regardless of whether she said it or not, that story showed conservatives and gays connecting in a modern pop-culture way. I thought it was awesome.

There was something that wasn't perfect about that night. Rumbling of trouble was starting to make its way to me. The anti-gay forces were starting to circulate the *Metro Weekly* article with the "nasty bigot" line, and they were accusing us of incivility and name-calling. (It's not name-calling when it's the word for it.) It was the beginning of the campaign to make GOProud the bad guys in the two-year CPAC sponsorship fight. That's right: over two years of attacks launched at us, and when we fought back, we were the bad guys. The next day we put out a statement in which Chris apologized to Cleta and we did our best at damage control.

The last day of CPAC was another very big day for us. We wanted to do something that everyone could agree benefited the conference. Through friends, we were able to make contact with Donald Trump, who was beginning to signal that he was considering a run for president. We invited him to CPAC and arranged for him to have time to speak from the main stage. He accepted.

Mr. Trump and his entourage arrived late, but after he spoke to reporters, they did make it up to our hotel suite for a few minutes before it was time for his speech. We had snacks and drinks there for them. Mr. Trump is a massive figure, both figuratively and literally. He's huge. He commands a room with his physical presence. He was definitely in command of the scene, but I was a bit surprised that he was not very talkative. The small talk seemed a bit forced. That's not what I expected from someone with his level of success. I expected him to be more engaging. We had some snacks and did our best at small talk. Then I saw Mr. Trump try to go into the bathroom, but it was occupied. The only other bathroom was the one in the bedroom. It was the bedroom where I was staying, and where we had thrown all of our mess to "quick clean" the suite before Trump arrived.

Of course he went into my room and into the bathroom. I was mortified. There were clothes strung everywhere, underwear on the bathroom floor, hair products and TV makeup all over the place, etc. . . . It was quite a scene, I was sure. When he came out of the bedroom, one of his staff handed him a hand sanitizer wipe that he used and then threw down in the middle of the floor. I thought that was weird.

Then, it was time to go. We all headed down the elevator and toward the ballroom where Trump would be speaking. I have to say that walking through a hotel lobby with Donald Trump and his entourage is something to experience, really something. The folks at the conference were totally excited to see him.

We were all hanging out backstage while he was waiting to speak. That's when I first met Rand Paul. He was the new senator from my home state of Kentucky.

I went up to Senator Paul and introduced myself. I told him that I was a Kentuckian and that I was born in Warren General Hospital in Bowling Green, where he was an ophthalmologist. He shook my hand and said it was nice to meet me, then just kept looking forward. He didn't even smile. I was surprised. He had no reaction to that personal connection with a constituent who happened to be backstage at CPAC with Donald Trump. He had no personality. Zero. Or it could have been discomfort with gay people.

He and his dad Ron Paul, who ran for president three times, have always pandered to the crazies, so maybe that was it. Both Pauls have aggressively courted social conservatives in their campaigns, including hiring socially conservative strategists to consult on their presidential campaigns in Iowa. Rand even went so far as to support the Federal Marriage Amendment in his race for the Senate in 2010. He has since backed away from that position, but in a 2015 interview, he said that he is "offended" by the fact that gays want to get married.

I thought that his personality wouldn't help his future in politics if that was the way he interacted with people on a personal level. That's especially true in the early presidential primary states, such as New Hampshire, where retail personal politicking is important. They don't like hardcore social conservatives in New Hampshire, either. He would still be doing Lasik in Bowling Green if his daddy, who is very personable and also more libertarian in his views, hadn't run for president so many times, I thought.

Trump brought down the house with his speech. We learned later that it was the most-viewed speech online of any at CPAC. Most people agreed that it was the biggest moment of the whole conference program. We were glad to have been a part of making that moment happen because that's all we ever wanted to do in the first place—help make CPAC better. We did.

When Trump was done speaking, we did the whole famous-person walk through the hotel's kitchen to a limousine waiting at the back door. Mr. Trump seemed like a different person after his speech. He was much more engaging and friendly than he had been in our interaction prior to the speech. One of his staffers said to me, "I'm glad that's over. You know, that was his first political speech." So that was it. That's why he was so awkward acting before he got on stage. He was nervous about his first political speech. Now he could loosen up a bit. I liked knowing that even Donald Trump gets nervous before a big moment like that.

Once we got Trump and his entourage off, I raced upstairs and into the bathroom. I wanted to see what Mr. Trump had seen when he went in there before we went downstairs for the speech. Actually, it wasn't that bad because the housekeeping staff had been in and straightened it up a bit. There was something unusual, though. There was a white hand towel on the sink with makeup on it. It was way too orange to have been mine. I surmised that Mr. Trump had gone in there to touch up his face before getting on the stage.

It used to be that political figures only wore makeup when they went to television studios for debates or interviews. These days, when you can have a camera in your face at any moment, it's much more common for politicians and public figures to wear at least a little powder to keep down the shine. It's the norm now. In fact, it's so common that many politicians' personal schedules include "HMU" (hair and makeup) every morning. So it was perfectly understandable for Trump to go into the bathroom for a touch-up, but if he would have just let us know, we would have had a team of Homocon helpers in there to help him look fabulous!

The other cool thing that happened that day was our friend Ann Coulter's speech at CPAC. We worked it out with Floyd and his security team to get one of our guys, Jon Fortin, up to the microphone during the question-and-answer portion of Ann's remarks. Ann's last question, right on cue, was our question about GOProud's inclusion in CPAC. Ann, as usual, hit a home run. She forcefully made the case for including gay people in the conservative movement. Gays should be conservative, she said. She again stressed that "just because you are born gay, doesn't mean that you are born liberal." Nobody could deliver that message to that audience better and more effectively than Ann Coulter. That was the cherry on top of what was, overall, a great week.

None of the Republican presidential candidates running for the 2012 GOP nomination addressed the controversy around our sponsorship or inclusion of gays in the party in their speeches at CPAC. They should have. That would have been a great opportunity to make a strong statement about the type of president they wanted to be, one that was everyone's president. None of them did it because they were afraid of negative backlash from the anti-gay, out-of-touch wing of the party.

David Keene's term as ACU's chairman came to an end at CPAC, and GOProud's run as a CPAC sponsor would soon end too. Al Cardenas, a lobbyist from Miami, became the new chairman. He had been against GOProud from the beginning.

After every CPAC there is a big meeting with all the cosponsors to discuss how the conference went. The meeting is usually a big bitch session about: not enough signage, the food, the schedule, and about seven thousand other complaints. In 2011, the post-CPAC cosponsors meeting was about GOProud.

Keene and Grover Norquist both reached out to me earlier that day to make sure I was planning on attending the lunch meeting. I was there, and so was everyone else—including ACU board members and the heads of many national conservative organizations. Nobody, it seemed, sent low-level staffers to attend on their behalf. This meeting was important. The lunch was a buffet catered by Chick-fil-A in the big meeting room at the offices of Americans for Tax Reform, the organization Norquist leads.

The meeting was led by David Keene. His successor, Al Cardenas, was sitting at the table next to him. CPAC Director and my good friend Lisa De Pasquale, who wrote about this meeting in her 2014 book, *Finding Mr. Righteous,* was on the other side of Keene, and Millie Hallow, a National Rifle Association executive and ACU board member, was next to Cardenas and directly across the table from me.

We all sat there eating our Chick-fil-A while Lisa and the ACU staff went through their summary of the event—attendance numbers, website hits, etc. They talked about what worked and what didn't work at the conference. It was the biggest, most financially successful CPAC ever. Donald Trump's speech was heralded as the highlight of the event. *You're welcome*, I thought, because we brought both the largest financial contribution and Trump to the table that year. Of course the anti-gay "boycott" didn't result in fewer attendees, in fact, it was the opposite—the most ever! The gays' involvement was good for CPAC.

I remember eating my dessert, a brownie, when the discussion of GOProud started. I looked over at Millie, who was "smoking" a chocolate flavored e-cigarette for her dessert, and she gave me a reassuring smile. I don't think either of us knew what was coming.

Then, one by one, a half-dozen or so people rose to speak against GOProud's inclusion in CPAC. Most of them accused us of being "uncivil" or "poorly behaved." Over the course of two years, we had endured countless attacks from them, and they found one thing we did while defending ourselves to point to as our "bad behavior." The "nasty bigot," or "name-calling," as they referred to it. I thought that they couldn't be serious, but they were. The lie they were spinning didn't seem to faze them.

Cleta was at the meeting that day, and it was clear that she had again coordinated the opposition against GOProud. Most of those speaking against us were her clients or known allies. I just remember her sitting in the first row of chairs away from the table, eating her Chick-fil-A with her paper plate resting on her knees, every now and then piping up to interject something negative about GOProud.

She didn't stand up and give a big speech, because that's not her style. Cleta rarely leaves her fingerprints. I have heard some stories about tactics she used in her opposition to us that would blow your mind, including advising her firm's political clients, in her professional capacity, to oppose GOProud. An ACU board member even showed me some of her email rants where I recall she said, in substance, that, "you just can't *trust* gays" and "gays can't be conservative."

There came a point in the meeting when I knew that I had to stand up and say something in our defense. I raised my hand and was given a microphone. I stood up and walked to the front of the room. Cleta was sitting directly to my right.

I had not prepared any remarks, but that was okay, because it was one of those moments when God just takes over. I still couldn't tell you exactly what I said, but I started by saying, "All we did was sign up for CPAC, because that's what conservatives do." I told the group about myself and my conservative principles and values. I told them about GOProud and our members' desire to be a part of CPAC. All we wanted to do was to be a part of CPAC and help to make it and the entire conservative movement better.

I said that we had done everything we could do to avoid the public fight over our sponsorship. I reminded them that, at Keene's request, I had not attended the planning meetings with all the sponsors to help craft the program. I didn't have a speaking role, like all of the other sponsors got. We did those things in order to keep a low profile, because Keene and others had hoped that would satisfy the opposition.

I then told them that maybe my taking a step back in order to avoid the fight had been a mistake. Maybe if they had seen more of me then they would better know me and know GOProud, and know that we belonged at CPAC because we were conservatives. I also reminded them that since we only work on federal issues, we had never even taken a position on whether states should enact civil marriage for gay couples. So don't pretend that the opposition to us was about gay marriage—it wasn't. The opposition to us was simply because of who we were. We were gay, and some didn't like that. I spoke for a few minutes, or it may have been an hour—I couldn't tell you.

When I was finished, I put the microphone down and returned to my seat. The room erupted with applause. Everyone except our detractors and the ACU staff and board was clapping. Some of the attendees were standing. My friend Christine Hall, from the Competitive Enterprise Institute, leaned over to me and said, "That was awesome! You didn't even stutter!"

When the meeting was over, I ended up in the elevator with David Keene and Al Cardenas. David put his hand on my shoulder and said, "Good job today." I exited the building and walked around the corner on the sidewalk in front of Macy's. Then I burst into tears. I cried like a baby right there in the middle of downtown Washington. I was completely emotionally drained. I left it all in that room that day.

The next morning I tweeted, "The best part about the whole thing yesterday was the Chick-fil-A for lunch. Love it." I did love the irony of that, since many of the gay liberals had advocated for a boycott of Chick-fil-A because of its founder's support for anti-gay causes and organizations. That day was one of my most memorable moments of staring bigotry in the face and confronting it head-on. And I did it all while eating Chick-fil-A.

During that time, I made an effort to reach out to various ACU board members in hopes of shoring up support for our inclusion in future CPACs. One of the new members of their board was former Hewlett-Packard CEO Carly Fiorina. I saw her as a potential ally because GOProud had endorsed her and had run television ads on her behalf in her failed US Senate campaign in 2010. We had even endorsed her over a pro–gay marriage Republican, California Congressman Tom Campbell, in the primary. Campbell was the first Republican US Senate candidate to publicly support marriage equality. We endorsed Fiorina because we didn't view her as anti-gay, even though she opposed civil marriage for gay couples, and she was the heavy favorite in the primary. I thought for sure that she would return the support we had given her now that GOProud needed her.

I made multiple attempts to talk with her, but her assistant repeatedly brushed me off and told me that Ms. Fiorina was just too busy to even take a phone call from me so that I could tell her our side of the CPAC sponsorship story. I knew that she was close to both Cleta and Cardenas, but I expected that she would show some loyalty to us because of our past loyalty to her. I was wrong. She wouldn't even take a phone call from me. I have no doubt that she sided with the bigots when it came down to voting the gays out of CPAC.

Many people reached out to me during Fiorina's 2010 campaign expressing disappointment that we would support her. The most common criticism of her that I heard then was that she was just a "bitch" personally and she didn't treat people well. I dismissed that because that's not an uncommon criticism of powerful women. I defended her, but in the end, I got a first-hand taste of the type of person Carly Fiorina is.

GOProud's star was continuing to rise. A few weeks after CPAC we had a high-profile fund-raising event at the Alexandria, Virginia, home of well-known GOP strategist Mary Matalin and her husband, former Clinton advisor James Carville. James wasn't there. He stayed at home in New Orleans, where they live full-time.

That night was pretty awesome. We hadn't planned a big huge program, just an intimate discussion. We had about seventy-five people in Mary's living room. Grover was there. Margaret was there. Ken Mehlman was there, and he said a few words. He had come a long way since managing George W. Bush's disgusting anti-gay campaign in 2004. We raised a good amount of money, got a little press out of it, and we continued to show the country that high-profile conservatives were engaging publicly with gays. This was good.

By the end of the summer of 2011, I was feeling really good about everything we had done with GOProud over the last two and a half years. We were on stable financial footing, and gearing up to play a role in the presidential race that was just about to really get going. I decided to spend a week at a friend's beach house on Fire Island.

Fire Island Pines is a place like no other. Its residents are mostly gay, and even though it's very close to New York City on Long Island, it feels like a world away. A carefree feeling sweeps over you when you get on the ferry and cross over the bay to the island. I needed that week. I needed to recharge from what had been an exhausting year so far, and I had to get ready for an even busier fall fast approaching. After a relaxing week off, I packed up on that Friday and headed into New York City.

I had a lunch date with a FOX News reporter, who had flirted with me when I was in the greenroom waiting for a TV hit a couple of weeks before, then I was going to head back to DC that afternoon. After my date, I was walking down Fifth Avenue window-shopping when Chris called. He said that the Daily Caller, a conservative news website, was reporting that GOProud had been kicked out of CPAC 2012, and that several reporters had called him asking for our reaction. I didn't think that could be correct because we had kept in pretty good contact with the ACU's executive director Gregg Keller and the rest of the ACU staff over the last few months. Even though our friend Lisa had been fired as CPAC director, in part because of her vocal support for GOProud, I thought we had a decent relationship with them. Surely, they would have called and told us if there had been a vote of the ACU board to kick us out. I also thought that David or Grover would have called to let us know what had happened.

I later found out that the ACU had emailed official notice to our general inquiry email account info@GOProud.org. That account was monitored by the interns. That day I had said that they could leave early because I was out of town and it was a hot summer Friday. So, no, nobody from the ACU contacted us to tell us that we had been kicked out of CPAC. We found out from reporters.

A couple of days later I was alerted to a *Miami Herald* report about a Facebook conversation involving Al Cardenas's wife. She went on an epic anti-gay rant on CNN commentator Ana Navarro's Facebook page. It was shocking. It was telling. This was what the Cardenas family really thought about gay people. No wonder we were kicked out of CPAC. We never had a chance once Cardenas took over the ACU board. It just took him a few months to get his ducks in a row before he let the guillotine fall on us.

I went to Grover's weekly gathering of conservative leaders, the "Wednesday Meeting," that next week. By then, I had regained my resolve and I wanted everyone to see me there. I wanted them to see that I wasn't backing down. When I arrived at the office I immediately ran into Keene. He and I went off to sit at a table on the side. He told me that many ACU board members were pissed at Cardenas because they didn't realize that they were voting on anything. They thought his email to everyone was a request for feedback and a survey of the opinion of the members of the board about GOProud, not an official vote.

Keene and I talked for a while. I showed him the printout of Mrs. Cardenas's Facebook rant. He looked at me and said that we should find a way to use that in some way against Cardenas. He also reassured me that we had done everything we were asked to do and the only mistake we had made over the two-year conflict was apologizing to that nasty bigot Cleta. He knew more than anyone what Cleta had instigated behind the scenes.

He had been a real warrior in the battle and he was as disappointed as we were at what had transpired.

I sat in the Wednesday Meeting just wondering what people in the room were thinking when they saw me. Lots of the folks there had been advocates for GOProud. Several of them came over to me to shake my hand or pat me on the back to again show their support. The one thing that none of them ever did, though, was condemn the anti-gay folks who were against us. Some of them said that the bigots were wrong, but nobody ever really stood up to them. Even though we were winning hearts and minds to our side, I could see that very few people were willing to include gays in the coalition if that meant losing the anti-gay folks.

About halfway through the meeting, Grover got up and had his chief of staff take over the meeting. A few minutes later, Grover's assistant came up to me and whispered that Grover would like to see me downstairs in his office. *Oh good*, I thought. I hadn't had a chance to talk with Grover since all this blew up. I knew he would be able to help. I bounded out of the meeting and onto the elevator down to Grover's office.

When the elevator doors opened I could see into the glass-walled library that was just outside Grover's office. I saw that Al Cardenas was sitting at a conference table with Grover. Sitting in the reception area was Grover's wife, Samah. She asked me to sit with her until Grover was ready for me. I told Samah that I wasn't expecting to see Cardenas. She just asked that I not kill him there! I told her that I had too much respect for Grover to soil his office with Cardenas's dead carcass.

Actually, I was glad that Grover was in there because I knew that he would be a good moderator. He's a smart guy, and he certainly has had a lot of experience from his many years in Washington at bringing feuding political factions together. A few minutes later Grover came out and asked me to come into the library. To my surprise, Grover wasn't staying. He held the door open for me and said, "Jimmy you remember Al, don't you? I'll leave you two alone to talk." Then he and Samah left for lunch.

There I sat across the table from the devil. Al Cardenas had been described to me by people who know him as a stereotypical straight, macho, Cuban man from Miami. Someone who knows him said to me, essentially, that he doesn't respect any of the personalities involved in the whole CPAC controversy because Cleta was a woman and we were gay, so none of us were at his level. He certainly never treated us with any kind of respect. That was most evident when he couldn't even pick up the phone to call me or Chris to tell us that he was kicking us out of CPAC.

I could feel the blood start to boil in my veins. You know, the kind of rage that starts building in your guts and moves up to your head until it comes out of your mouth and you say something you wish you hadn't said, or worse, you do something you shouldn't do. I wanted to lunge across the table and strangle the fucker. That's the kind of rage I was feeling inside at that moment, but I just kept thinking about what I had just told Samah. *Don't kill him, you promised Samah.* That was my mantra.

Cardenas started to explain to me that what Chris said about Cleta just couldn't be tolerated and that's why the board called a vote. I asked him about the several board votes about GOProud that we had barely survived over the last two years before that comment. "What was the problem then, Al? It's because we are gay. No other reason than because we are gay." *What shouldn't be tolerated was the rank bigotry*, I thought.

He started to tell me about how he has always had gay friends, and that there are gays in their family. I interrupted his "some of my best friends are gay routine" and looked at him with disdain and said, "I read your wife's Facebook rant." He shut up for a second. I think he was stunned that I would stand up to him. He wasn't used to that happening to him. Then he started in about how conservatives oppose gay marriage, that's the conservative position. I then reminded him that GOProud didn't have a stated position on marriage. It was because we are gay and he knew it. He just looked down.

I already knew that he had gay people in his family. In fact, I knew of more gays in his family than he did. One of the things that happened over and over again when I was running GOProud was that people would contact me with stories of closeted gay activity among conservative figures. That happened when I worked at Log Cabin, too. Chances are that I've heard all about it if it happened. That's why I knew that former Senator Larry Craig was guilty of allegedly soliciting sex from an undercover cop in a Minneapolis airport restroom. The story in Washington was always that if you wanted a meeting with Senator Craig, just go to the Union Station men's room. So when Al Cardenas was elected chairman of the ACU, I received calls from more than one person telling me of their man-on-man activity with a member of the Cardenas family who happened to be married to a woman.

Cardenas found the "nasty bigot" comment and used that to kick us out. It's important to note that no gay organization, including GOProud, has been allowed to cosponsor CPAC since 2011. Both GOProud and Log Cabin Republicans have attempted to become sponsors in years since. I got up and headed to the door. I turned around and looked at him and told him, "There will be consequences for your actions, and you won't like them. You'll deserve whatever comes your way." I didn't know if the worst of those consequences would come in this life or when he had to explain himself to Jesus, but I knew that there would be negative consequences for actions like this. I felt just like Whoopi Goldberg's character, Celie, in *The Color Purple,* when she leaves her husband saying, "Until you do right by me, everything you even think about gonna fail!" Then I stormed out.

The receptionist smiled and whispered to me as I passed, "Good job." I got on the elevator and headed back to the office. By the time I got back to the office, political news sites were already reporting about the meeting. Reporter Ben Smith reported that "it didn't go well."

No, it didn't.

6

PRIMARILY CRAZY

It didn't do any good to dwell on being kicked out of CPAC—the presidential race was gearing up in full force. We didn't need to be a part of CPAC in order to demonstrate that the gays were part of the coalition. The 2012 presidential race was the biggest national stage, and that's where we would show that we were team players. First we had to navigate the primary, then we could jump on board in full support of the Republican nominee.

It was tough for us because it was a crowded Republican primary, with a field of mostly social conservatives. The front-runner was a candidate we could support as the nominee: Mitt Romney. The fact that I had found him completely unacceptable in 2008, and that now he was the best option, just demonstrated in vivid detail the cultural backslide the GOP had been on since 2004. The leading presidential candidate had reversed his previously held positions, and, just as important, had reversed his previously inclusive rhetoric on social issues to win the nomination.

We knew that we would spend most of the primary campaign on defense, and dealing with anti-gay "eruptions" from the field of candidates, who would surely attract unfavorable attention and misstep in their zeal to appeal to the anti-gay segment of the party. We had already engaged in a few public controversies concerning some of them.

One such controversy that seemed to set the tone for our whole primary campaign experience involved Michele Bachmann. Bachmann was a Minnesota congresswoman who, before she was in Congress, made her mark in the state legislature as a single-issue legislator, being anti–anything gay-related. Anti-gay marriage, anti-nondiscrimination laws, she was just all around anti-gay. In 2009 she smartly pivoted away from her anti-gay agenda and embraced the message of the Tea Party. She was a darling of the Tea Party and advocated for rolling back the size and scope of government, but of course she hadn't changed her anti-gay views—she just wasn't making that her focus during the rise of the Tea Party. The problem for us was that we had a lot of friends and supporters in the Tea Party movement who were supporting her. We had to be very careful in our criticism of her anti-gay, outside-the-mainstream views, because much of her audience was our audience too.

Michele Bachmann and her husband Marcus own psychological counseling centers. Their centers counsel gay people on how to become straight. They administer the so-called ex-gay therapy, the practice of using prayer and counseling that some claim turns gay people straight. There was controversy in the news about their family business, because that type of therapy has been widely discredited as quackery by the psychological community. It's actually psychologically damaging to people. Bachmann had also gone back to beating the anti-gay drum and restated some of her old outside-the-mainstream views about gay people.

GOProud issued a public invitation to sit down and talk with her. We wanted to show her audience, and our shared audience, that we were there to help. We knew that public engagement with us would help her, but it would help us more. Honestly, her staff and consultants were decent to deal with behind the scenes, even though the meeting never actually happened. Chris and I both did a lot of television and other interviews about it. I appeared on MSNBC with anchor Thomas Roberts, where he asked me why we would want to even meet with Bachmann, because she wanted to "extinguish" gay people. The video of that interview went viral because he used an inflammatory and biased word like "extinguish." I got a lot of criticism because I hadn't more forcefully pushed back on Thomas's statement, but the truth is, the nature of her business is to "extinguish" homosexuality. That was a harsh word for him to use, but not untrue. It was exactly the truth.

During that time I made a trip to New York City for a couple of television hits. Margaret Hoover had a new book out, *American Individualism: How a New Generation of Conservatives Can Save the Republican Party*, so there was also a party for her there. I got a haircut in Washington before I got on the train to New York. I told my hairstylist all about the Bachmann situation, and that I needed the haircut because I was going to be on television. The stylist was an immigrant from Tunisia who had just been there to see her family, so I wasn't sure how up to speed she was with the latest political news in this country, and I "overly explained" the situation. A few days later, I got a surprising phone call.

Well-known national political reporter Molly Ball called the office, and I happened to be the one who answered the phone. She said, "Jimmy, I have a strange question for you." I remember asking her if I would need to call her back with an answer after she asked the question. She said, "maybe." She went on to ask, "Were you in a Dupont Circle hair salon on Monday? Did you say that Michele Bachmann was crazy and nuts? Did you say that Marcus Bachmann was a 'flamer' and 'ex-gay faggot'?" I was stunned. I was shocked that beauty parlor gossip would be treated as a real political story, but I knew that I had said that and it would be very damaging to GOProud if it got out.

It has been widely speculated, but never confirmed, that Marcus Bachmann is an ex-gay and a product of the type of ex-gay therapy that their counseling centers administer. I think I also told my hairstylist that he was like Remington electric shaver's Victor Kiam, "Bachmann liked it so much he bought the company!" I told Molly that I would call her back. Chris and I powwowed about it. We called our lawyer who advised that I get a public apology ready. I called Molly back and lied to her. I said that "I categorically deny that I said anything about Marcus Bachmann." It was far less damaging that I called Michele crazy, but for me to call Marcus gay (or a flaming faggot!) would have been a big story, and it would hurt our organization.

I certainly learned a valuable lesson about talking too loud in public places in Washington. I think it was the guy who was getting his haircut in the chair next to me who was Molly's source. I remember seeing him look over at me a few times. I thought he was checking me out. I was wrong. He was eavesdropping. That's the only time I have ever knowingly, flat-out lied to a reporter, but after just having been kicked out of CPAC, our organization couldn't survive a scandal like that. Fortunately, Molly didn't write a story about it. A couple of weeks later, Bachmann won the Iowa Straw Poll, which placed her firmly in the top tier of candidates running for the GOP nomination.

The fact that she was leading the pack in Iowa showed me just how powerful the anti-gay folks in the party still were. In fact, they still are today. Their power, especially in places such as Iowa, hasn't diminished in the least.

Chris and I were careful not to repeat the same mistake that we were part of at Log Cabin four years earlier when Rudy Giuliani got the reputation as being the "gay candidate." Or at least, we didn't want a candidate to get that label because of us. For the most part we were impartial. We worked to develop good relationships with all the campaigns' staffs and sought meetings with most of the candidates. Eventually various members of our board, including Chris and me, would announce our personal support for various candidates, but we intentionally spread GOProud's support around to different candidates in the primary. The board members who publicly supported candidates all supported different ones.

A lot of gays were supporting former Utah Governor John Huntsman, and some of his senior people reached out to me about getting on board in a formal way. They wanted me to work to raise money for the campaign from gay and pro-gay Republicans. I was a fan of his conservative record as governor, but when I had the opportunity to see Huntsman in person that summer, I hadn't been impressed. I just didn't think that he was engaging and personable enough to get elected president. Even at a small, intimate barbecue at his home in Washington, he just seemed kind of plastic to me—not real. I passed on the opportunity to get on board with Huntsman, but maintained a good relationship with the campaign. I would not have been disappointed if he had ended up with the nomination because he and I were in sync on most policy issues, and I liked his tone.

That fall, Chris ended up in former Godfather's Pizza CEO Herman Cain's camp. We had a really great relationship with his staff. In fact, it was one of the best relationships we had with any of the candidates or their staffs. I think that was because Cain wasn't a conventional politician like the other candidates were. He didn't care that anyone might see him engaging with gay people. He was natural and authentic. That's what I liked about him.

One of my favorite GOProud stories from the whole 2012 campaign was something that I wasn't even there for. Chris had gone to Las Vegas to speak at a conference, and he was able to arrange a meeting with Cain who was also speaking at the conference. Cain had just been involved in a week- or two-week-long story in which he had been asked if he would appoint a Muslim in his cabinet. He said no. Then he clarified that they would have a higher level of vetting to make sure they weren't connected in any way to Muslim extremism. Then he was asked if he would hire a gay. He said yes, if they were qualified. Those answers sparked more questions from reporters that Cain just didn't answer as well as he should have. Anyway, it had been a distracting story that he couldn't get rid of.

When Chris met with him they talked about that. Cain admitted that he hadn't handled it well in the media, but he meant what he said. He leaned over to Chris and said in his Georgia accent, "The last time I checked, the gays wasn't flyin' planes into buildin's!"

Former New Mexico Governor Gary Johnson was especially awesome to work with. He was the only candidate who actually supported legal civil marriage for gay couples. He wasn't doing well in the polls and had trouble even getting invited to all the debates, so he wasn't likely to be a contender for the nomination.

That was too bad, because he was a really nice guy. Johnson was a good friend to GOProud. He had been at the Big Party we had at CPAC with Andrew Breitbart, and he showed up to anything we asked him to come to. We even had a "GOProud Town Hall" event in New Hampshire that he came to. I would have been happy to see him elected as president, but it just wasn't within the realm of possibility, given the political dynamics of the GOP primary that year. The forces had lined up against him, and the truth was that Johnson's "live and let live" attitude on social issues was just unacceptable to that powerful segment of the GOP who don't like people who aren't like them. He just wasn't where they demanded he be on issues such as marriage, abortion, and marijuana legalization. Even on immigration, an issue that he had directly dealt with as a governor of a border state, he wasn't hardline enough for them.

I went to several of the presidential debates. I also traveled to Orlando for the FOX News debate that was part of a big conservative conference in September. A lot of people I knew were there. In fact, I was on the plane with Ryan Sorba, the young man who had denounced GOProud from the stage of CPAC a year and a half before. He was seated directly in front of me, then moved to the seat next to me on the plane. We shared a Diet Coke. Really. It was a bizarre flight. I was just glad when the plane landed in Orlando.

It was a good thing I was there for the debate, because some of the questions were asked by average citizens via YouTube, and one of those questions came from an openly gay service member. The question was directed to former Senator Rick Santorum, who is notoriously known as one of the most anti-gay Republican politicians in the country. When the service member finished asking Santorum about his support for rolling back the repeal of Don't Ask, Don't Tell, a position that was also held by several other candidates, some members of the audience began to boo. I was appalled and embarrassed because conservatives in the crowd actually booed a member of our Armed Services.

Santorum did not acknowledge or thank the questioner for his service to our country, nor did he condemn the booing; he just launched into an outrageous anti-gays-in-the-military answer, in which he said gay service members were seeking special privileges (not true) and that gays serving in the military was a "social experiment." It was outrageous. We immediately put out a statement, and the next day I ended up doing radio interviews with talk shows set up on the conference's radio row. By coincidence I was on radio row at the same time as Santorum. He would do an interview, then I would, or vice versa. He was always perfectly nice when our paths would cross on the campaign trail. Chris and I ended up on a plane with him to New Hampshire before a presidential debate at Dartmouth College; he was totally nice to us, but obviously, Santorum winning the nomination was one of our worst-case scenarios. His views were just too far outside of the mainstream.

We did finally get a chance to "meet" Michele and Marcus Bachmann at another debate that fall. GOProud was a sponsor of the Western Republican Leadership Conference in Las Vegas, and there was a CNN debate as part of the conference. Chris and I had great seats for the debate, right up front with all the candidates' spouses. (For the record, I did catch Marcus Bachmann staring at me a couple of times during the commercial breaks. I don't know if it was because he recognized me, or if he thought I was cute!)

After the debate, everyone was just kind of milling around. We chatted with Texas Governor Rick Perry and Rick Santorum, then we saw Bachmann. She and Marcus were on the stage, and Chris and I were standing right up next to the stage. Chris got her attention and she bent over to talk with us. Chris introduced us and said that we were from GOProud. I'll never forget her response. Marcus was standing behind her with his hands on her hips as she was bent over to talk to us. Then she said in her Minnesota accent, "Ohhh. Well God bless you!" That was it. The entire content of GOProud's big meeting with Michele and Marcus Bachmann.

Rick Perry started out with a message in his campaign that I really liked. He was touting his record of creating a climate for job creation in his state. He called it the "Texas miracle." In truth, Texas was one of the only states that was doing well economically, and it was exactly the message he should have been running on. The problem for him was that he wasn't gaining traction with that message. That was especially true in Iowa, where Bachmann's anti-gay message vaulted her into contention. Perry had to do better in Iowa if he was going to get the momentum to make it to the primaries in later states.

Most of his campaign's senior staff were longtime staffers and part of his inner circle in Texas. By late November 2011, Perry demoted some of his Texas-based team and brought in new senior advisors who had national reputations and presidential campaign experience, including new pollster Tony Fabrizio and media strategist Nelson Warfield. I knew Tony from his work to advance marriage equality. He is an openly gay man who had done a lot of work for Log Cabin, liberal gay philanthropist Tim Gill, and several state-based pro-gay efforts. One of our advisory council members, strategist Liz Mair, was also part of the Perry team. I felt confident that if Perry ended up the nominee, despite his past anti-gay statements, that he would run a campaign, with a pro-gay staff, that we could support. I was wrong.

There were a couple of things the Perry campaign did that raised red flags with me. The first was a blistering news release they put out criticizing Secretary of State Hillary Clinton for giving a speech raising the issue of gay rights at a UN conference in Geneva. There was nothing in Clinton's speech that anyone, even anti-gay Rick Perry, should have disagreed with. It was carefully crafted for an international audience, including countries in the Middle East, for crying out loud. Perry blasted her for raising the issue on the international stage. I have always thought that religious extremism and brutal dictators in some parts of the world, particularly the Middle East, are the greatest threats to gay people in the world. I was thrilled with Clinton's speech, and I was shocked that Perry would condemn it.

I reached out to Liz Mair, who said that things inside the campaign were taking a disturbing turn since Fabrizio and Warfield had taken over. She said that it appeared that jobs and economic growth in Texas were taking a backseat to cultural issues in an effort to play to the social conservatives in Iowa. I was surprised, given Tony's sexual orientation and history of pro-gay activism, that he would be advising such a shift.

It was only a few days later that the new strategy concocted by Fabrizio and Warfield would come to be fully revealed. They unveiled Perry's new ad, "Strong," in Iowa. The ad featured Perry talking directly to the camera saying, ". . . there is something wrong in this country when gays can serve openly in the military, but our kids can't openly celebrate Christmas or pray in school." Outrageous, I thought. I couldn't believe that he would say that patriotic Americans, who happen to be gay, are what's wrong in America. I wasn't the only one. The YouTube video of the ad went viral and it was roundly condemned as out of bounds.

Everyone knows that ads don't make it to television without the pollster's intimate involvement in creating them. Every word in any campaign ad, especially at the presidential level, is carefully chosen based on polling data. I knew, like I knew that the earth was round, that Tony had been a part of creating that horrendous ad. I told Sam Stein, a reporter with the Huffington Post who was writing a story about the ad, that I was disgusted that a gay man, who had spent much of his career working on pro-gay campaigns, was now playing both sides of the culture-wars in order to collect a big fat check from an anti-gay presidential campaign.

After a phone call with Liz, it was clear that the backlash against the ad wasn't going to cause Tony to resign from the campaign. By the end of the day I was fed up. So I took to Twitter and unleashed a few emotion-fueled tweets in which I said that I was tired of "faggots" lining their pockets with anti-gay money while throwing the rest of the gay community "under the bus." I made sure that everyone knew I was referring to Rick Perry's new pollster. Chris also chimed in on Twitter. He was as outraged as I was.

That night Sam Stein, who was finishing up his story, emailed me to confirm that Fabrizio was openly gay, and I told him that was like asking me if I'm openly gay. I only knew Tony in the context of gay Republican activism, so of course he was openly gay. Besides, he's lived with his partner for as long as I've known him. Stein told me that Tony was trying to get him to kill his story because he wasn't "out." That was total bullshit. It was just a ploy to keep the story from going up. It's a rule in politics that consultants and staff members shouldn't be the story. Tony was just trying to keep from being the story.

The next day, Sam's story came out, in which Tony claimed to have been against running the ad. There were other stories out that day too, accusing me and Chris of "outing" Tony—even though he wasn't "in." There was a firestorm of criticism aimed at us from the right. The biggest critic was Breitbart, who quit our advisory council over it. (We later made amends and worked together again.) He said it was because he had always been against "outing." Again, I didn't know Tony was in, I just thought he was a money whore who was willing to compromise his principles to make a buck. I still think that about him.

It wasn't until about ten months later, when Austin political reporter Jay Root's book, *Ooops! A Diary from the 2012 Campaign Trail,* came out, that I was vindicated. Root was able to get copies of campaign emails from senior Perry aides in Texas, who had been somewhat sidelined by Fabrizio and Warfield, that confirmed what I knew to be true. The new anti-gay strategy of the Perry campaign was conceived by Warfield and Fabrizio together, and was part of their effort to revive Perry's sinking campaign. They had overruled Perry's Texas advisors to implement the new strategy. Needless to say, it didn't work.

As it got closer to the end of the year, it was becoming clear to me that Mitt Romney would likely be the nominee. Paul Singer hosted a huge fund-raiser for Romney in New York. Singer had stayed on the sidelines for much of the primary because his favorite potential candidates, Chris Christie and Paul Ryan, had passed on getting into the race. Now he had settled on Romney. It was pretty clear that everyone was going to end up settling on Romney. So I wrote a check to the campaign and I went to Singer's event. Everyone else there maxed out their contribution, but because of our relationship, Singer's staff allowed me to attend with only a $250 check. That was all I could afford. It was over $200, so my contribution would be publicly reported, with my occupation and employer, in the campaign's end-of-year finance report. I was ready to go on the record as supporting the least bad candidate in the race.

When the end-of-year finance reports came out, my contribution was listed with my name, but mysteriously, my occupation and employer were listed as "requested." I thought that was strange because it was Singer's staff who collected and tracked all the money from that event, and they knew exactly where I worked. That's the reason I was there! I wondered, did the Romney people want to hide the fact that the head of GOProud, the gay group, was supporting their guy?

For months, I had made many repeated attempts to develop a relationship with the Romney campaign, and several times requested a meeting with Romney. My outreach to his assistant Kelli Harrison and others was rebuffed by the campaign. I chalked that up to their being ultra-cautious in the primary, but intentionally not reporting my contribution correctly seemed a little extreme to me.

We were a little concerned a few weeks later when Rick Santorum edged Mitt Romney to win the Iowa caucuses. Fortunately, anti-gay wacko Bachmann didn't end up getting enough votes in Iowa to stay in the race, but damn, the Santorum surge was a huge concern to us. It was more and more clear that we needed Romney to win. I never thought that I would think that after the 2008 campaign, but he was by far the least of all the evils that had any momentum leaving Iowa.

I wrote an op-ed for The Daily Caller in which I personally endorsed Romney. It was my individual endorsement, not GOProud's official endorsement. We still had various board members in different camps, but it was important for us to use the weight of my endorsement to signal to our people that we were ready to get on board with the guy who would more than likely be the nominee.

We took a group of folks to New Hampshire for the primary in an effort to use that national stage to demonstrate that gay conservatives were part of the conservative movement and engaged in the Republican primary process. I had a brainstorm that we should host a "Homocon-tinental Breakfast" the day before the primary election in the Manchester Radisson Hotel. That hotel was ground zero for media covering the campaign. My friends Ellen Ratner and Audrey Mullin, with Talk Radio News Service, were coordinating the "radio row" in the hotel, where all the candidates and surrogates would come to do radio interviews. It was on the second floor of the hotel. We had our breakfast set up on the mezzanine just outside of radio row, and it overlooked the hotel's lobby and seating in the restaurant. We couldn't have had a more visible place in the whole country that day.

We had signage all over the hotel's lobby and mezzanine advertising our free continental breakfast. We had coffee, fruit, bagels, and the usual continental breakfast stuff. We also had GOProud branded coffee cup sleeves, like you get at Starbucks and other coffee places so you don't burn your hand on the paper cup. Before we knew it, you couldn't go anywhere in or around the hotel without seeing the GOProud coffee cups! It was great marketing. It was also a terrific opportunity to interact with candidates, surrogates, and staffs from the different campaigns. The Romney people still kept their distance, though.

Later that day our group went to the Romney office to volunteer to help get out the vote for Romney. They thanked us, gave us some stickers and told us that they had plenty of help.

We left. They clearly didn't want people wearing GOProud caps working in their office that day. We didn't even get into the victory rally the next night. We were in the overflow room. Romney won New Hampshire.

We had a GOProud board meeting in New Hampshire and voted to endorse Romney if he won the South Carolina primary, which was the next contest after New Hampshire. We figured that the nomination fight would be all but finished by then because nobody else would have the money or momentum to go on. By that point only Romney, Santorum, and Newt Gingrich were really left in the race, and Romney was the only one of them with any money or organization. Perennial candidate Ron Paul was still around, but most people, myself included, never thought he was a serious candidate.

Bruce Carroll was our board member who was supporting Newt Gingrich. That turned out to be a good thing, because Bruce lived in South Carolina and Gingrich was surging there, and ended up winning the South Carolina primary. So, GOProud held off on officially endorsing Romney because his inevitability was in question after his embarrassing South Carolina loss. The anti-Romney vote wasn't dissolving as fast as Romney had hoped, I'm sure. It was clear that this primary would go on for a while longer, with Romney, Santorum and Gingrich still in the hunt.

Gingrich wasn't as bad as Santorum on the gay stuff, but the thrice-married candidate had said some things about gay marriage that would cause us problems if he were the nominee. Even though Romney was only marginally better, I still hoped for Romney to pull it out because I thought that once he won the primary, he would do what he did to win the governorship in Massachusetts. When he won the governor's race, Romney had aggressively courted gay voters, which in turn showed straight urban and suburban voters that he was an inclusive leader. I knew that Gingrich and Santorum would continue a hard right course on cultural issues if they had the nomination. At least with Romney there was hope, based on his history. A nominee who showed a broad, inclusive campaign was the only way the Republicans could hope to win. Modern demographics demand that inclusiveness is demonstrated by showing that nobody is excluded. I was hopeful that the Romney people understood that. At least I thought they were more likely to understand that than the other campaigns.

The next few weeks were tortuous. The race was very unstable. Up and down. Gingrich and Santorum. We tried to come up with a strategy that could lead us to an endorsement of the nominee, but it was getting harder and harder because all three candidates were pulling hard right in their effort to secure the nomination. The anti-gay rhetoric was impossible for us to defend. Nevertheless, we did everything we could to position ourselves so that we could endorse the nominee and be good team players, regardless of who it was.

One way we started to make the case for our support of the eventual nominee, whoever it was, was that we put out a statement with GOProud's 2012 agenda. It highlighted tax reform, Social Security reform, and combating global anti-gay extremism. We picked issues that the eventual nominee could support, or at least support the concept, if not the specific proposal. We had to show that the eventual nominee was a perfect fit for our organization, even though it seemed that every week one or more of the candidates had something to say about gays that made me cringe.

That was the longest spring I can remember. I just wanted it to be over already. I was getting less and less thrilled with every

Romney attempt to pander to crazies, to assure them that they could support him. It came down to Gingrich and Santorum as the last two standing against him. I was still pretty confident that neither of them had the money or infrastructure to secure the nomination, but the longer they stayed around, the more Romney would have to concede to the social conservatives in order to win.

Gingrich dropped out, but Santorum was still up and running because he still had the backing of well-known megadonor Foster Freis. Now, I just prayed that Romney could put Santorum away, because the longer Santorum held on, the more power he would have going forward. As the runner-up, he would wield tremendous influence, particularly at the convention, and now he was even a potential running mate.

Santorum eventually did concede the race to Romney, which was a huge relief. I was still concerned about what influence Santorum and his supporters would have on Romney going forward. It made me very nervous.

The whole primary process was a huge wake-up call for me. GOProud had been wildly successful at our core mission of demonstrating common ground and an inclusive conservative movement, but getting kicked out of CPAC and being kept at arm's length by Romney, among other things during the primary, had my hope fading. The power that the forces of intolerance had on the right was not diminishing at all. I only hoped that things would change now that we were moving into the general election campaign.

I was a twenty-one-year-old College Republicans activist, who cheered on Pat Buchanan's famous culture-war speech at the 1992 Republican National Convention in Houston, Texas. This photo of me with the US Senate candidate who ran in South Dakota that year, Charlene Haar, was taken at that convention.

Pictured here (far left) as part of the national staff of Log Cabin Republicans, in the organization's happier and more successful days, with former California Governor Arnold Schwarzenegger, just after he had voiced his opposition to the anti-gay Proposition 8 that was on the ballot in California in 2008.

Jimmy the Tea Party gay! 2010.

I love this photo of my friend, conservative author Ann Coulter, and me. It really shows her personality. Ann is a total sweetheart, and that doesn't always come across when she appears on television.

A scene from GOProud's "Homocon 2010" event at the home of technology entrepreneur Peter Thiel in New York City. (Left to right) KABC Radio's John Philips, the side of my friend, CNN commentator Margaret Hoover's head, me, FOX News's Andy Levy and Greg Gutfeld, and the back of Bill Schultz's head.

The artwork, by the cartoonist Sarjex, we used to promote Homocon 2010, featuring the "Right Wing Judy Garland" Ann Coulter!

My political partner in crime, GOProud cofounder Chris Barron, and me toast our success at the coffee shop that was near our office on Capitol Hill.

GOProud made history during the 2010 midterm elections as the first national gay organization to run television ads against Democrats. Our ad, "The Real Democrats of DC," was a hilarious spoof on the opening credits of the popular television franchise, *The Real Housewives*.

I'm addressing the crowd at GOProud's Big Party at CPAC 2011 with Andrew Breitbart. GOP mega donor Paul Singer's political and philanthropy advisor Annie Dickerson is looking on with The Daily Beast's John Avlon and CNN commentator Margaret Hoover in the front row.

Conservative media mogul Andrew Breitbart speaks at GOProud's Big Party. Chris Barron (right) and I (left) are on either side of him.

Grammy-nominated singer and songwriter Sophie B. Hawkins chats with former Republican National Committee chairman Michael Steele after she performed at GOProud's event. That's when she allegedly said that she didn't refer to herself as a conservative, but she'd f**k Sarah Palin!

The cover of the LGBT magazine *Metro Weekly* that depicted Chris Barron and me riding a pink elephant came out the week of CPAC 2011. That's the issue in which Chris referred to Foley & Lardner attorney Cleta Mitchell as a "nasty bigot."

Working in my hotel suite at CPAC 2011 just before Donald Trump arrived.

Greeting CNN producer Evan Glass (left) and reporter Jim Acosta (right) as they arrive to interview Donald Trump.

Walking through the hotel lobby with Donald Trump and his entourage at CPAC 2011. That was back when he was just beginning to venture into the political arena. I certainly didn't know then the path he would eventually take on several controversial issues.

Speaking at a GOProud fund-raising event in the home of famous GOP strategist Mary Matalin. Former RNC chairman Ken Mehlman (left) had just said a few words too. That was during the time, after coming out as gay, when Mehlman was on his "apology tour" for running the anti-gay 2004 Bush reelection campaign.

I have no idea what I said to Mary Matalin (seated) or why she reacted with a hand over her mouth. I just know that I was so grateful for her hosting the pro-gay 2011 GOProud fund-raiser in her home in Alexandria, Virginia.

That's me on radio row in the Manchester Raddison the day before the 2012 New Hampshire primary.

The scene at GOProud's fabulous party at the 2012 Republican National Convention. We always tried to show that Republicans were cool and hip, and in touch with modern culture. That event, complete with go-go dancers, definitely conveyed that message!

This reporter asked me why the Romney campaign did not send a speaker to the GOProud event. I was stuck. I didn't want to tell her the *real* reason.

I ran into some of the same demonstrators who had protested our GOProud event the night before on the street in Tampa, Florida, during the 2012 Republican National Convention. I decided to get a picture with them, since, as they put it, HOMO SEX IS A THREAT TO NATIONAL SECURITY!

During a commercial break during the *Piers Morgan Live* show in the CNN Grill at the 2012 Republican National Convention. *Time's* Joel Stein is next to me while host Piers Morgan talks with a producer. Piers just couldn't believe that there was a gay who supported Romney…. by then, I was starting to wonder the same thing!

My friend and former CPAC director, Lisa De Pasquale, and me at a GOProud event in 2012. Lisa was an important heterosexual ally and she risked a lot to stand up for gay conservatives.

The panel on the *Wanda Sykes Election Special* on Logo TV in October 2012. The guests with Wanda Sykes standing behind us (left to right) Hilary Rosen, Joe Solmonese, Amy Holmes, and me. Funny how I was so far out to the right in this photo!

Playing the role of "the gay for Romney" on FOX News Channel's *Fox and Friends* with host Gretchen Carlson the morning after a presidential debate in October 2012.

Political reporter Kevin Cirilli interviewing me in front of the US Supreme Court in 2013 on the day of the oral arguments in the Proposition 8 and DOMA cases.

My announcement that I left the Republican Party received a ton of media attention. This was an interview I did about why I left the GOP with ABC News's Rick Klein (right) and Yahoo News's Olivier Knox (middle).

7

GAYS FOR MITT

It was such a relief, after months of uncertainty, when Mitt Romney finally secured enough delegates to win the Republican nomination. After months of having my support pushed into the closet by the campaign, I was looking forward to actively working with them to help make the conservative Romney palatable to average Americans.

I expected that after spending the entire primary season kowtowing to the anti-gay, culturally out-of-touch crowd, that the campaign would be excited to finally be able to show that Romney was in touch with real life in 2012. It was a no-brainer for me to think that they would want some type of very public engagement with members of the gay community, because gay people are a real part of life in America now. Public engagement would help to show Romney as a culturally modern and inclusive leader. That would also balance out all of the public appearances he made with anti-gay leaders, including speaking at the Family Research Council's conference, during the primary campaign.

GOProud was the perfect fit for that because I had already personally endorsed him, we had solid conservative credentials, and we weren't asking for any policy changes or concessions in exchange for our support. We were on message with his campaign's theme, too—what the gays care about is jobs and the economy. We were already poised to officially endorse him, but it would have been helpful for us, from a public relations standpoint, to have some sort of engagement, preferably a meeting, ahead of that.

Our support would help him, but it would help us too. We knew, from firsthand experience, what happens when you don't endorse the nominee. Both Chris and I worked at Log Cabin in the years after 2004, when Log Cabin did not endorse Bush's reelection because of his support for the Federal Marriage Amendment. Log Cabin was completely shut out by Karl Rove and others at the White House after Bush won. That's what happens when you upset the others and go against the groupthink on your team. They box you out. We were determined not to be in that position again, because we knew how important it was to have a gay voice with access to the White House when it was needed. Romney was facing an opponent with a failed economic record, and he had a good chance of winning.

It was equally important for Romney to publicly acknowledge our contribution, and now it was time to ask for that. The Romney campaign had kept us at arm's length for months, rarely acknowledging my attempts to engage with them. Now I expected a partnership of sorts. It was time for them to engage with us. For me, it seemed like a no-brainer, a win-win situation.

Back in 2000, after Bush had secured the nomination, he met with the Austin 12 group of openly gay Republicans in Texas. Bush emerged from that meeting and spoke to the press, saying he was a "better person" for having met with the group. That helped to solidify his credentials as a "compassionate conservative." I knew that Romney needed some sort of moment like that, too.

I reached out to the deputy campaign manager, Katie Packer-Gage, and asked for a meeting with top campaign officials in hopes of eventually securing a private meeting with Romney and some sort of public event with the campaign. Based on my experience over the last six months, I thought it was unlikely that Romney would do a joint news conference or anything similar to the press event that Bush had done with the Austin 12 in 2000. They were too afraid of backlash from the crazies for that, but a private meeting with him and something public with a surrogate or senior staff seemed like a reasonable request. Actually, I thought it was a minimal request.

I would have even been happy with a private, off-the-record meeting, and the ability just to say that we had met Romney before we endorsed him. I got a phone conversation with Katie. Seriously. A phone call with the deputy campaign manager was all they were willing to do. No meeting with the candidate.

A friend of mine who grew up in Michigan with Katie had briefed me about her ahead of my call with her. My friend is a longtime Republican operative who had spent time working in the political trenches with Katie. He thought that I should exercise a bit of caution with Katie. He said that while he wouldn't characterize her as "anti-gay," she did come from a hardcore evangelical Christian background and was very plugged in to the social conservative world. Once Romney secured the nomination, he hired most of Rick Santorum's senior staff, so the campaign was full of the crazies. I knew that their point of view was well represented inside the campaign, and from what my friend told me, Katie was one of them too.

The call with Katie was one of the strangest conversations I've had in politics. She grilled me about GOProud's and my conservative credentials, asking "What do you consider conservative?"

After all of the media attention we had received over the last few years, I didn't know that there was anyone on the right who didn't know about us. She acted as if she had never heard of us. I'll never forget the condescending tone in her voice when she said, "What does the word 'conservative' mean to you, Jimmy?" I obliged her with an hour-long history of our organization and my background.

It was a pretty humiliating phone call. I felt like a child being talked down to. Katie talked to me like this was my first day at politics school. The whole time I was thinking that I could teach her a thing or two.

I thought, doesn't she get it? Doesn't she understand that the rest of the country thinks Mitt hates gay people and I was giving her a painless way of proving that he doesn't? Was the whole campaign so out of touch with modern culture that they didn't understand how important that was to do?

In the end, Katie said that there would be no meeting with Romney because the campaign didn't want to look "etch-a-sketch," a reference to a gaffe made a couple of weeks earlier by the campaign's senior strategist Eric Fehrnstrom when explaining how the campaign would shift away from pandering to the crazies and essentially start over now that the general election had begun. It didn't matter that we weren't asking for any changes in Romney's anti-gay policy positions. The mere appearance of talking to gay people was a bridge too far for him.

Romney was in a good position to beat President Obama because of Obama's failed record and Romney's background as a competent manager and businessman, but it was important for him to gain trust and connect with people on a personal level. Romney had to find ways to prove that he cared about all Americans. The problem the Romney campaign had, and the problem Republicans have today, is that only focusing on issues that affect everyone, such as jobs and the economy, ignores the fact that some issues uniquely affect some people and not others. Only focusing on the issues that affect everyone shows that you only care about issues that affect you, and that you lack the ability to see things from another perspective, or even recognize that people who aren't like you face challenges that you don't. Talking about those issues that are unique to some of us doesn't mean the politician is playing "identity politics"; it shows their ability to see things from other perspectives. The ability to empathize is the most important characteristic a politician can demonstrate in today's multicultural reality. Too many on the right fundamentally lack that ability.

Obama couldn't run his campaign on his economic record, so he would have to run it on cultural issues and portray Romney as an out-of-touch, straight, rich, white guy. Engaging with gay Americans was a great way for Romney to counter that. I couldn't get it through Katie's head how important it was for Romney to show that he wasn't the anti-gay homophobe the Democrats wanted to portray him as. Then it dawned on me. Maybe I was wrong about Romney—maybe he was truly a homophobe.

I started to think that Romney's pro-gay, inclusive record and rhetoric as governor was just an act in order to get elected in liberal Massachusetts. I began to see that he was, at his core, really an anti-gay bigot. I had heard stories about Ann Romney not being comfortable with gay people, and now I was starting to realize that maybe Mitt wasn't either. That just had to be the real issue, I thought.

That was the beginning of my doubts about Mitt Romney as a person. I was starting to think that maybe there was something to the Democrats' assertion that the Romneys didn't care about anyone who wasn't like them. Sure there are lots of public examples of the Romneys' generosity toward other straight, white Mormons, but there is little on record to show any diversity in their compassion. He further confirmed my suspicions about him with his speech at Liberty University, the school founded by the anti-gay culture warrior, the late Jerry Falwell. I was disappointed that he would even speak there, and it seemed to me politically stupid for him to do it after he had secured the nomination. He was where he was comfortable. He was in his element at what is considered the mother ship of the anti-gay industry. I watched the speech on television and it was clear that he was with his people there at Liberty, and his people didn't like my people. That appearance sent a clear message to people like me: we weren't part of Mitt Romney's vision of America.

The same message was sent by Texas Senator Ted Cruz in March 2015, when he launched his 2016 presidential campaign at Liberty. Then he went on to make his opposition to gay marriage a centerpiece of his campaign. His America doesn't include everyone, either.

We went ahead and endorsed Romney without a meeting because we felt we had no other choice. It was time to get on board. I was just grateful that I at least had Katie as a relatively senior level contact in the campaign, because I knew there would be times when we would need each other. I mistakenly thought that she would see that when it happened.

The left pounced on the announcement of our endorsement. Gay sex and relationship columnist Dan Savage took to Twitter to call us "house faggots," a reference to the days of slavery when "house slaves" worked in the slave owners' house. The implication was GOProud members had a good life "in the house" and were willing to support the status quo to preserve their good life in the house, whereas the "field slaves" desired freedom because their life, working in the fields, was harder. It sparked a round of news stories and prompted Taiwanese animators to create a hilarious web video that pitted the house faggots of GOProud, who were portrayed shining Romney's shoes in the house, against the "morally superior field faggots" who worked picking cotton on Obama's plantation. The video was, frankly, awesome.

The liberal television hostess Joy Behar of *The Joy Behar Show* said that our endorsement could have been because ". . . the GOProud guys are just attracted to Mitt Romney's sons . . ." *Village Voice* columnist Michael Musto said, among other things, "You're like Jewish Nazis! Black Klan members!" Other prominent liberals attacked us too. I began to make the rounds defending our endorsement on television and solidifying my role as the de facto gay spokesman for Mitt.

We had a joke in our office, "Gay conservatives take it from both ends!" That was certainly true that year. The liberals called us traitors to the gay cause, and the hard right just thought we were evil sinners and wanted no part of us. The 2012 campaign showed me, almost more than anything else, that there probably was not a place for me in the traditional political arena. The endorsement announcement was just the beginning of what was becoming clearer to me.

It was only a few weeks later that I would get another taste of the anti-gay reality of the Romney campaign. My friend Ric Grenell was hired as the foreign policy spokesman for the campaign. Ric, an openly gay conservative, is a longtime Republican operative and well-known foreign policy expert, having served as the United States spokesman at the United Nations for eight years. Of course, the crazies went nuts! A gay in the campaign! Oh dear! Publicly and privately, behind the scenes, they attacked. The public line from the campaign was much different from the ugly reality that happened behind the scenes.

Ric is one of the sharpest and most witty people I know, and his Twitter feed reflects that. When the opposition began to rear its ugly head against him, most of the anti-gay conservatives who opposed him were too savvy to publicly admit that their opposition to him was because he was gay, so they pointed to controversial tweets as what made him an unacceptable spokes-man for Romney. Most of the opposition began to dig into Ric's social media posts to try to build a case against him, rather than publicly object to him because of his sexual orientation. A few, such as the American Family Association, were upfront and honest with their bigotry, stating that Mitt couldn't have a "homosexual" advisor because he would be secretly lobbied to support gay marriage.

I reached out to both Katie and Ric via email to offer assis-tance when the story of the controversy broke. They both assured me that it would blow over if nobody fanned the flames of the story. I laughed to myself. If you just keep your head down, it will blow over. I knew better. I was pretty sure that the behind-the-scenes drama with this situation was much more intense than was being portrayed in the media—just like it was with us and CPAC.

Ric was hired on a campaign staff now populated with many of Santorum's top aides. The anti-gay social conservatives had many direct lines to the top, and I knew that they would use them. I knew that lying low and hoping it would blow over wouldn't work with those people, because nothing is ever enough. They wouldn't relent until they had Ric's head.

After several days of ducking the issue, Romney finally said publicly that Ric was hired because of his qualifications, or something generic like that. It was a weak response to a reporter's question, and just the bare minimum of what Romney should have done. I was disappointed, because it was the perfect time for Romney to stand up and have his "Sister Souljah moment," much like Bill Clinton did with the radicals in his party in 1992. That's what he needed to do to show America that he wasn't one of the extremists. It's pretty simple: when you don't stand up and denounce the bigots, then people are left to think that you are just like them. This was his opportunity to stand up and show America that his GOP was a new, modern party, just like Clinton did for the Democrats in 1992. The reality was that it wasn't a new, modern party. Mitt's party was stuck in the anti-gay past. He didn't have the desire or backbone to withstand the pressure from the opposition.

A few days later I got an email from Ric giving me and others a heads-up about a story that was about to break. He had quit the campaign. He had been sidelined there and didn't feel like he had any other choice but to leave. He wasn't fired or asked to leave, but he wasn't being allowed to do the job. He was hired as a spokesman, and was told to remain silent on calls with reporters and kept out of sight. He couldn't allow that to continue, so he resigned.

I was devastated. It was very emotional for me, because that was a moment of clarity when I realized the hell I was going to face over the next five months. I knew then what Romney was made of, and I had just had an ugly taste of what we would be put through in our support of him.

I called the office of our biggest donor, Paul Singer, who was also one of Mitt's biggest funders. I told them to get ready for calls from reporters and others about the situation. I knew they would get calls because of Singer's high-profile support for both gay rights and Romney. I also asked for help reaching the campaign's top people above Katie's level, because I thought that if we went over Katie's head, perhaps to campaign manager Matt Rhodes or others who might have been closer to Romney himself, then maybe we could get to a less dismissive decision maker who would listen to us and accept our help in dealing with issues like this in the future.

The response from Singer's staff was as disappointing as Katie's had been. They had bought the campaign's explanation that it was the Twitter feed, not Ric's sexual orientation, that made him controversial. Being the good establishment Republicans that they were, Singer and his staff fell in line with Mitt's party line—any excuse to ignore the problem of homophobia in their ranks.

Anyone who is gay knows that there is a different standard for us. That's especially true on the right. I remember Andrew Breitbart, during the "nasty bigot" controversy, telling me that there was a higher standard for us. In this case, an edgy Twitter feed is a badge of honor for most in politics, but not the gays. The gays' existence is already controversial enough. Don't push it.

Chris and I often said that conservatives were thrilled to have us on their team as long as we knew our place, didn't disagree, and fell in line. As soon as we stood up for ourselves and challenged the established rules, we were out, but "not because we were gay." We certainly had that experience with CPAC, and now Ric experienced his own version of what I call the every-reason-except-that-they-are-gay takedown.

I knew after this experience that we were on our own during this campaign.

One talking point I often used to make the case for how a gay person could be a Republican and not automatically a Democrat was that while there were significant differences between the two parties, and Democrats were more "pro-gay" than Republicans, both sides officially opposed marriage equality for gay couples. That helped me to make the argument about how conservative policy proposals, especially for tax and entitlement reform, were especially good for gay people. The bottom dropped out of that argument on May 9, 2012, when President Obama announced his support for legalizing civil marriage for gay couples in an interview with then closeted gay ABC News anchor Robin Roberts.

It was only about a week or so after Ric had left the Romney campaign, and I was still smarting a bit from that. I was in knots over the Roberts interview. On the one hand, I was elated the president of the United States had used the most powerful platform in the world to endorse marriage equality. On the other, I knew we had to find a way to criticize the announcement in order to be a Romney team player.

We knew that reporters would call us for GOProud's reaction, so Chris took the lead on the response because he was not really identified as a Romney supporter, even though he was on our board and voted for endorsement. He wouldn't be pressed like I would about Romney's position, and frankly, his statement wouldn't carry the weight that one from me would. We put out a written statement in which Chris congratulated Obama on coming around to former Vice President Dick Cheney's position on marriage, now that it was politically advantageous for him. Then we tried to keep our heads down. Of course, we were inundated with calls from reporters. We were also flooded with calls and emails from GOProud members and donors. We did our best to manage it by simply directing everyone to the written statement.

This was another perfect reason for the Romney campaign to want to showcase our support, but there was silence. They ignored us. Meanwhile, the Obama campaign and liberal super PACs were spending tens of millions of dollars to define Romney as the out-of-touch elitist that he was. Romney was doing nothing to counter that assault.

GOProud didn't have the resources to combat the attacks on Romney. In fact, I was getting concerned about our financial situation. Our fund-raising had been in decline for months. The whole spectacle of the anti-gay stuff in the presidential primary campaign and our being kicked out of CPAC had zapped the enthusiasm of our membership, and this new position from Obama only made matters worse. We made an effort to convince some Romney donors that it was in Mitt's best interest to have high-profile gay support to push back against Obama's culture-based attacks. Meanwhile, the Romney campaign was essentially (not specifically) telling everyone to pay no attention to our argument, that this campaign was about jobs and the economy, not about social issues. It made fund-raising tough, because our entire brand was built on being the gays who were on the inside of the conservative movement. That was a hard case to make to donors now that the Republican nominee didn't want anything to do with us.

8

FAKING IT FOR MITT

The general election campaign was shifting in to full gear, and it was time for us to engage and trumpet our support for Romney, even if he didn't want us to. I made the budgetary decision to focus our resources almost entirely on our presence at the Republican National Convention, happening at the end of the summer in Tampa, Florida. The thought of going to Tampa to be Romney's gay cheerleader made me nervous. I was worried that we would be shut out there as well, but we really didn't have a choice. I did have reason to be optimistic, though.

Back in January, Chris and I had visited with RNC Chair Reince Priebus and his deputy chief of staff Sara Armstrong in his office on Capitol Hill. It was a pretty good conversation because they seemed to understand the importance of showing an inclusive coalition. They were impressed with our work and asked that we have a visible presence at the convention, which of course was what we wanted too.

Chris and I had first met Reince at a cocktail party in Las Vegas after that debate where we had our encounter with Michele and Marcus Bachmann. He came up to us and introduced himself and said, "Everywhere I go I hear about the great work that GOProud is doing." His assistant Wells Griffith chimed in, "He's right, everywhere we go, people are talking about you guys!" They seemed to really get it and understand how our work was helpful to the GOP.

Reince and Sara made sure that GOProud was in the system to receive guest passes, hotel rooms, and all of the things that they did for other conservative organizations. They especially wanted us to have a large event one evening during the convention. We told them that's what we were planning.

Reince said, "You all have to have a big party! Do you think you can get Lady Gaga to perform?"

We were planning a big event with big name entertainment. I had already been to Tampa a couple of times to start planning it. We had a reputation to uphold after the famous events we produced featuring folks such as Ann Coulter, Andrew Breitbart, and Sophie B. Hawkins, but I did tell Reince that Lady Gaga was not likely. He seemed to understand the important message that was sent to the country whenever GOProud hosted a big event, and that it was especially important for us to do it at the convention.

I did set out to find some big name entertainment, but heard "no" from one agent after another whose star didn't want to perform at a GOP convention event, even if it were a gay event. We would focus on getting political celebrities to show up. That would bring star power and show the public embrace from the right that was critical to advancing our mission.

Anyone who has ever planned logistics for a group at a national political convention knows how hard it can be, not to mention expensive. The convention would be our biggest expenditure all year, and fund-raising was challenging in a post-marriage-supporting Obama era. The gays' wallets had closed, and the straight donors were in the process of being conned by Karl Rove to give to his centralized independent expenditure organizations. So there wasn't much money left on the table for us to go after. Some of the big GOP donors whom Chris and I asked for money told us that they thought GOProud's work could spark backlash and harm Romney. That was clearly what Romney thought. I couldn't think of a more important effort to fund to push back on Obama's culture-based campaign. I seemed to be the only one who thought that.

The RNC assigned us rooms at a Holiday Inn Express in Clearwater, about a forty-five-minute drive from the convention. It was less than ideal, but we took what they gave us without complaining because we didn't want to appear to be problem children. I was just grateful that they had given us twelve guest passes/credentials for the convention. That meant that everyone in our entourage would get to see at least part of the convention. We had about twenty-five folks in the GOProud group at the convention.

One thing that happens prior to national political party conventions is that different groups start to share and trade credentials and hotel rooms. There is always lots of last-minute shuffling. All of the different coalition groups were pissed off because we all ended up with really bad seats in the convention hall. Ours were worse than most. We were in the uppermost level behind the stage, out of sight in the nosebleed section.

I was especially surprised that the campaign hadn't included at least two good seats in our packet for Chris and me. The reality was that he and I were well-known figures and couldn't be seen sitting in the seats they gave us because that would have been reported in the media. I spent most of the convention sessions hanging out in the CNN Grill or one of the hotel bars in the area so I wouldn't have to wander around the convention hall without a respectable place to sit.

The convention was to start on Monday and end on Thursday, and our event was on Tuesday. As soon as we hit town I was running around at a hundred miles an hour working out our logistics, making sure that everyone got where they needed to be, and talking with reporters. I was the de facto gay spokesman for Mitt, and I was in high demand all week with national and international media outlets there.

The convention was canceled on Monday because of Hurricane Isaac, but that didn't stop the media requests. I did a ton of interviews that day—mostly from our hotel.

Our event on Tuesday was coming together except for one significant thing. We didn't have a big name speaker confirmed. The Romney campaign flatly told me no, they wouldn't send a surrogate from the campaign. After begging, I finally got Joshua Baca, the campaign's coalitions director, to agree to come, but I didn't have any famous person. I didn't know this for a fact, but I suspected that it was an official directive from the campaign, because within forty-eight hours of the campaign denying us a big name surrogate, several of the prominent figures that I reached out to and invited independently declined the invitations. Some of those invitations had been on the table for months, and it was just too much of a coincidence that they all declined within a couple of days of each other, after the campaign denied us a surrogate speaker.

I had also invited a ton of well-known conservatives and members of Congress to attend as "special guests." We had a good number of well-known conservative activists and media personalities listed as "special guests," but not a single member of Congress accepted the invitation. We were producing a very expensive event for about a thousand people, and it was at Reince Priebus's request, and I was surprised that they couldn't see how important it was to support the event and the message that it conveyed.

I was a wreck on the day of our party, and ran around all day like a crazy person getting ready for the event. We only had room for 1,200 people and we had more than 1,800 on the guest list, but it's common at RNC conventions for people to RSVP for every event, then not go to all of them. I was still worried that we wouldn't have room for everyone.

I practiced the remarks I had prepared for that evening over and over in the mirror. It was a speech that I had to give. We were at Romney's convention, and I was there to show that we were behind him 100 percent. I was getting nervous. I was hopeful that I would be convincing, and not look like I was just reading the words on the page. I knew that there would be a ton of reporters there. I had to be good. I was on edge about it.

I got a real boost of confidence when I walked into the venue we had rented for the event. It was the biggest gay nightclub in Tampa's trendy Ybor City neighborhood, and it was totally decked out for the party. I had worked for months with an event planner and the venue's management to make sure that the GOProud event was the best party at the convention. It was spectacular. There was no other event at the convention that was as awesome as ours.

We produced a first-class event to show that the Republican Party was cool and hip, and that even the gays were supporting Mitt Romney. We had gorgeous male and female go-go dancers in tight t-shirts that said "Freedom is Fabulous." There were dozens of disco balls hanging from the ceiling, and the guests got to take home disco ball key rings to match.

It was just the message that a candidate and a party that appeared culturally out of touch needed to send. It cost a fortune, but it would have been worth every penny if there had been some sort of engagement from the campaign. There wasn't.

We did, of course, have protestors. Fundamentalist Christian zealots demonstrated across the street from our party. They held signs that said we were going to hell, and that we were an abomination and an evil that had infiltrated the Republican Party. We actually didn't mind having them there. It just created more attention for us, and that attention showed that not all conservatives were like them.

We had approximately a thousand people there, including about two or three hundred reporters and media folks from around the world. Some of the biggest names in the conservative movement and in conservative media attended. Except, in the end, nobody from the Romney campaign or the RNC could bring themselves to come by and say thank you. Joshua Baca didn't show up.

Chris kicked off the program that night with nice remarks about our friend the late Andrew Breitbart, who had passed away earlier that year. Then I got the microphone for our keynote. Yup. Without a big name speaker, I was the big speech that night. It was all on me to get out there and tout our support for Mitt. My hands were sweating like fountains. The event planner had not arranged for a proper podium and microphone, so I was holding a handheld mic with my soaking wet hands. Despite having half an inch of powder on my face, I was shining like an oil slick because of the nervous sweat I was suffering from. The speech was fine. I did it. Just like I always did. Team player.

The reporters who were there reported exactly what we wanted them to report. Gays cared about jobs and the economy, and that's why they supported Romney. I did have to spin and deflect to a couple of reporters who asked me point blank why Romney hadn't sent anyone to speak at our event. I couldn't have the truth out there in the media in the middle of the convention. It would have been bad for us and horrible for Romney. Although I have to admit that I secretly hoped one of the reporters would write the story about the lack of support from Romney. I just didn't want to be blamed for a story like that, so I dodged the questions by pretending that we didn't really expect the campaign to send anyone to our event because our event "wasn't about Romney." Of course it was. Again, I compromised my integrity to uphold the Republican code.

By then, Chris had made the decision to personally support our friend Governor Gary Johnson's campaign, and was even advising that campaign as a consultant. Johnson had left the Republican Party and was the presidential nominee of the Libertarian Party. Chris left Tampa the next day to attend a meeting to make sure that Johnson got on the ballot in the District of Columbia. I was jealous. I wanted to get on that plane with him. All I wanted was to get the hell out of there.

The morning after our big convention event, I attended a breakfast meeting hosted by Grover Norquist. It was a take on his normal weekly Wednesday Meeting. Since I usually go to the Wednesday Meeting, I made a point to attend this convention edition of it. Joshua Baca, the Romney staffer who didn't show up to speak at our event the night before, was there too.

I approached Joshua and let him know how unhappy I was that he didn't show up the night before. His excuse was that there was a crisis with a surrogate for another event that he had to deal with. "I had a thousand people there and Mitt couldn't send anyone to say thank you for your support!" I said, "I've been fucked over by the Romney campaign over and over again. You have to make it up to me." He said he would but I didn't believe him.

On the last day of the convention I got up and called to check in with Chris. I asked him if he had seen me on CNN on *Piers Morgan Live* the night before and if he had any feedback. He had. He said, "Everything you said was perfectly fine, but you have *got to, got to, got to,* be more enthusiastic! You have got to at least pretend like you like the son of a bitch!"

I told him that it wasn't easy being the gay for Mitt. I said that I felt a lot of empathy for Ann Romney. Now I knew what it was like to "fake it" for Mitt!

After the convention was over, I took an extra day in Clearwater to go to the beach. I watched all the old saggy retired people walk past me, and I prayed for the strength to make it through the next two and a half months. I hoped I would make it through so that someday I too could walk this beach as a carefree retiree. Of course, I wouldn't be so saggy!

I knew that things in the campaign had been bad, but I was sure that the worst was yet to come. I just hoped that I could make it through without being called out as the fraud that I was starting to feel like I was.

I had to remind myself over and over again that it wasn't about me, and it wasn't about Mitt Romney. Our mission and our movement was much bigger than a few personalities. I was representing others, and working to build a movement. I moved forward with my work.

The following week would be my first Democratic National Convention. It was in Charlotte, North Carolina, and I was exhausted from Tampa, but lucky enough, through my friends Ellen Ratner and Audrey Mullin with Talk Radio News Service,

I got a couple of hotel rooms and credentials. I knew that the Democrats would turn up their volume on the cultural issues, and it would be important for me to be there to counter their attacks. Ric Grenell ended up using our other hotel room and passes in order to do the same thing in his wheelhouse of foreign policy. Even though he wasn't on Romney's staff anymore, he cared about his career and knew the importance of being seen as a team player in the politics business. We both went to Charlotte to show that we were on a team that had made it clear that they didn't want us.

Ric and I were disgusted by the rat trap of a motel that we were staying in, but fortunately there was plenty going on to keep us out and about. The CNN Grill became my refuge yet again, for a second week in a row.

Honestly, the Democratic convention's atmosphere was better. The setup and logistics in Charlotte were way better than Tampa. The Dems also seemed to be happier and having more fun. Their convention had real excitement and energy. Although I didn't agree with their policies, I couldn't deny that they had something the GOP convention didn't, but I couldn't put it into words. The RNC convention had a negative vibe. I guess it was because the opposition to Obama created negativity that wasn't countered with any optimism. Or it could have been the fact that different factions of the GOP's untenable coalition couldn't stand to be around each other, and it showed.

The other big difference was the diversity. There was a little bit of everyone there, some more than others. Actually, the visual contrast between the two conventions showed the clear difference between a diverse urban party and a white rural party. There were tons of gay people, black people, and other demographic groups represented at the Democratic convention.

It looked as diverse as America, and it projected an inclusive image on television. The Democrats' urban diversity was in stark contrast to the Romney convention that was a sea of old white people. Seriously.

My prediction was correct: the Democrats beat the cultural drum at their convention. This inevitably led to their win. They highlighted their diversity with speakers who focused their remarks on how issues affect different groups of Americans uniquely because of who they are and how they live. I had tried unsuccessfully, multiple times ahead of the GOP convention, to make sure the RNC included at least one or more openly gay speakers at the Republican convention. I was hammered with reporters' questions about why many other demographic groups were represented on the GOP stage, but not a single openly gay speaker. There has not been an openly gay speaker at a Republican convention since Jim Kolbe in 2000. Now, at the Democratic convention, there was one gay person after another on the stage—including the woman who would go on to make history as the first openly gay person elected to the US Senate, Tammy Baldwin.

The Democrats got it. The Republicans didn't. Showing gay people and other diverse groups as part of their coalition, on and off the stage, demonstrated that they were truly living real life in America today. Of course it wasn't just the gay stuff, but the multicultural connection in general that demonstrated to America that they got it. They understood the emotional and personal component that the vote for president carries for most Americans. The Republicans didn't. That's the way to demonstrate to Americans, including the normal people and independents, who may not agree with you on every single political issue, that you understand where they are coming from.

Then they are more likely to trust you to make the decisions about all the issues in the future that we don't know about yet.

My experience at the Democratic convention, more than almost any other single thing that year, convinced me that there was no way Romney could win. The Republicans didn't seem to have the ability or desire to connect with anyone who didn't already identify with them politically and, more importantly, culturally. I began to have doubts about whether the Republicans would ever win a national election again if they didn't understand this fundamental cultural reality.

9

47 PERCENT

After the conventions, I headed to New York to be part of the *Wanda Sykes Election Special*, which was going to air on Logo TV, the gay cable network. Not surprisingly, the Romney campaign refused to send anyone to participate in the show, so the producers reached out to me. I was a guest on a panel talking specifically about issues affecting LGBT people, and also the abortion issue. The other panelists were Joe Solmonese, a cochair of the Obama campaign and former head of the Human Rights Campaign; Hilary Rosen, CNN commentator and well-known Democratic insider; and Amy Holmes, an independent conservative commentator who hosts a show on The Blaze network. Amy was the other right-of-center person on the panel. Openly gay comedienne Wanda Sykes, the show's host, moderated the panel discussion.

The dynamic in the greenroom was interesting. The show's other guests included MSNBC anchor Thomas Roberts, then Congressman Barney Frank, former Bush White House official Brad Blakeman, and a couple of others who joined the show via satellite. Roberts and Frank both had their then fiancés with them. (Both couples later married.)

Barney Frank wouldn't speak to me or Brad Blakeman, the other Republican in the room. This was only the second or third time I had been around Barney in person, the first being at the Washington Sports Club on Capitol Hill, back when I still worked at Log Cabin. That "meeting" happened when he followed me into the sauna where I was wrapped in a towel reading the paper. He was not wrapped in a towel and he came on to me. He was completely inappropriate, even after I told him where I worked. He wasn't as excited to meet this time! Since then, of course, I had beaten him up in the press and we had run ads against him in his last reelection effort. He ignored me the whole time we were taping the show. I purposely stood by the food table in the greenroom to make him come near me. I knew he wouldn't be able to resist the sandwiches and cookies—everyone navigated toward the snack table.

Our panel was the last segment taped. The segment went fine, but I was nervous because we taped for a long time for what would end up being a short segment. I was a little worried about what the editors would do to me. I knew they would probably make me, the Romney guy, look bad, but I shrugged it off. Honestly, by then, I didn't care that much about that. At that point I was just going through the motions, really.

We finished up the taping and were back in the greenroom. Hilary Rosen and I were in the makeup area wiping off some of the "war paint," as we called it. She looked at me and said, "Poor thing. It must be hard for you."

What she said hit me like a ton of bricks. I just wanted to reach out and hug her and burst into tears. I was thinking, *You have no fucking idea how hard this is!* I didn't do that. I don't think that she's a hugger, anyway. What I did say to her was something like, "We'll all be glad I've done this if Mitt wins. I'll be the only gay with any shot at talking to his White House." I knew that was a lie. I knew that a President Romney wouldn't be any more inclusive of gay people than candidate Romney, so there really was no point in my doing what I was doing.

I was getting better and more careful in my messaging when I talked to the press about Romney. I didn't lie or say something I didn't mean, but that was getting more difficult to pull off. I focused on Obama's failed record, the poor economy, and the need for Romney's management skills in the White House. I quit pretending that I thought Romney cared about people or that he could empathize with Americans who were struggling. I didn't think he did. The problem for Romney was that America wants their president to care about them, whoever they are. That's why Obama was elected president in the first place. He gave us "Hope," remember? That's also how Bill Clinton won, and George W. Bush was "compassionate." I knew that the heartless venture capitalist, who only cared about other rich, white, straight people had no hope of getting elected, but I kept up my act just in case I was wrong.

I continued my attempts to engage the campaign. I reached out to them ahead of the debates and told them that I would be on hand in the debate cities to respond to Obama's continued assault on Romney on social issues. I told them that they should use me in the post-debate spin rooms when the reporters questioned surrogates on cultural stuff, so they could then direct them to me, the gay, to tell them that what Americans care about is jobs. The campaign ignored my multiple offers to do that.

Chris and I flew out to Denver for the first debate anyway. We decided to stay in the hotel where the ACU was having a regional mini-CPAC conference. Even though we were banned from ACU events, we knew that a lot of our conservative activist friends would be there. It would be another good opportunity for conservative influencers to see us engaged in the campaign and as the team players we were.

There we sat in our hotel rooms in Denver, unable to attend the debate where "our candidate" was debating or the conservative conference happening across the lobby from us. We did our best to use social media and I did interviews with some reporters to try to show we were there as a part of the effort to elect Romney. We spun it like the pros we were, and our audience continued to think that we were rock stars and that we were actually full-fledged members of the team. That's what you do when you're doing your best to be a team player, but inside it was humiliating for me. We were just pretending to be on the team. The team had made it clear what they thought of us.

Romney's performance in the Denver debate was stellar. It energized me, just like it energized everyone on our side. I was starting to rethink my assessment. I was starting to think that maybe, just maybe, he wasn't a total moron. Maybe he could win this election.

Then the next day, Romney made a surprise appearance at the conference a few hundred feet from where Chris and I were working in the hotel lobby. I still didn't meet him.

I was still obsessed with getting some sort of public engagement with the campaign, because it was important. I had gotten to know a senior campaign strategist and surrogate, Bay Buchanan. I had the opportunity to sit next to her and visit with her a couple of times at Grover's Wednesday Meeting. She was a famous television commentator and campaign manager for her brother Pat's past campaigns for president. So I reached out to Bay.

My email to Bay laid out the case for engagement and invited her to be the special guest and campaign surrogate for

GOProud's "Unity" reception. That reception was something that I hadn't planned on doing, but if Bay would do it, then I would find the money and throw it together.

Bay is one of the smartest people in politics, and she got it. She immediately accepted the invitation, but expressed a bit of surprise at being asked since she is known for being a social conservative. I thought that she was the perfect surrogate for a "unity" event precisely because she was a social conservative. I suspect that she hadn't run the idea up the flagpole with the campaign before she accepted the invitation, because in subsequent emails that I was copied on between her and Joshua Baca and others, it was clear that the GOProud event didn't rate very high on the priority list. Nobody else from the campaign showed up to that event, and I even saw the email where Bay specifically said to Joshua that he should be there too.

We threw together a little reception with about eighty or a hundred folks to show up for cocktails in DC. Bay was awesome. She and her husband couldn't have been nicer, and they stayed the whole time interacting with everyone there. We got a good amount of press out of it too, including from several international reporters who attended. I was relieved to get that accomplished.

The next debate was just outside of New York City on Long Island. I again told the campaign that I would be available to be a surrogate in the spin room. I thought it would be especially important with this debate, because it was a "town hall"-style format, with questions from the audience. It also only focused on domestic policy issues. I was absolutely sure that someone in the audience would ask a "gay question."

I was so sure that I reached out to the FOX News Channel's executive vice president Bill Shine and asked to be booked on their morning show, *FOX and Friends,* the morning after the debate. One thing I knew from my previous conversations with Roger Ailes, the founder and CEO of FOX News, was that he understood how culture impacts politics and I knew he understood the importance of showing that the gays were on the team. It would especially be important for me to be out front after the gay stuff was discussed during the debate.

Again, the campaign kept me away from the debate. I watched it from a hotel room in midtown Manhattan where I went to bed early in preparation for my FOX hit the next morning. I was wrong, as it turned out—there was no gay question during the town hall.

There was, however, a question asked of Bay in the spin room after the debate, because reporters ask questions about things that voters are talking about and care about, even if it's not what the campaign wants to talk about. She now seemed to be the go-to person in the campaign on all things gay, after having just appeared at our event in DC. I don't think she counted on that happening when she agreed to come. A reporter asked her about Romney's position on gay marriage, and she misstated it. She said that he thought it was a state issue, which I thought should have been his position at the time, but it wasn't. Romney actually supported the Federal Marriage Amendment, so the campaign had another round of stories about marriage, and they had to walk back Bay's comments by reaffirming Romney's actual extreme position. That wouldn't have happened if they had had GOProud there taking the questions.

The next morning in FOX's greenroom, I was talking with former Senator Al D'Amato (R-NY), who was appearing on the show before me on a political panel to discuss the debate. He told me he had a hard time getting a pass to the debate from the campaign. He said he'd had to tell them that he was going on FOX in the morning in order to get to attend. I told him that he must have been more convincing than me because that reason hadn't worked for me when I asked the campaign for a ticket to the debate!

★

More people in America watched that debate on FOX News than on any other television network. That meant that their viewership of *FOX and Friends* the next morning was huge because televisions were already tuned to FOX from the night before. The interview went great. I talked about how gays were supporting Romney because of jobs and the economy.

That TV hit was great for us, because FOX's audience was just the audience we needed to reach. I had been on that show just before the convention too, but this interview was bigger. Our office got a ton of great feedback in phone calls and emails from people who saw me on television. The love from FOX viewers that day was what I really needed. It reminded me that our mission was to influence the culture on the right, and we were doing that.

As we got closer and closer to Election Day, the boost in the polls from Romney's first debate performance was fading, but many GOP strategists and pollsters went on television to predict a Romney win. They were citing polling data that contradicted the majority of national and state polls, because many of their polls used different turnout models than the majority of polls. They were wrong. They weren't talking to the same people I was talking to during my travels all over the country, that was for sure. I thought that they must have overestimated the number of committed Republicans and underestimated the number of independents and Democrats who would turn out to vote in their polling, because it was clear the momentum was tilting in Obama's favor.

All of it, from the events over the last year to the crazy predictions of a Romney win, started to make sense to me when the famous 47 percent video came out. Romney had been secretly recorded explaining to a group of donors that approximately 47 percent of Americans weren't even going to consider voting for him, so his campaign wasn't even going to pretend to seek their votes. That would be a waste of their time.

I could add up all the demographic groups and socioeconomic groups that probably made up his 47 percent. Romney gave the example of people who rely on government assistance as a group of people in that number, but there were others too. I worked backward to approximate the groups of people the Romney camp thought they needed to vote for him in order for him to win. I added, based on past performances by Republican presidential candidates, the percent of the vote they hoped to get from various demographic groups and geographic locations. I also tried to estimate the number of independents the campaign hoped to get. I knew right then, that he probably considered gay people, who make up approximately 6 percent of voters, to be part of that 47 percent. He wasn't making any attempt to get our votes at all. What he didn't seem to consider is that 100 percent of Americans have gay people in their lives, and since all politics is personal, issues affecting gay Americans are personal to everyone, no matter what demographic groups they happen to belong to.

The 47 percent comment was very, very damaging to Romney. He truly didn't want everyone's vote, because he didn't need everyone's vote. He only cared about 50 percent plus one, and he couldn't be bothered with talking to the unwashed masses in the 47 percent who didn't fit into his "win equation," because his time was too valuable to waste on those people. The rich, white, straight, old people who made up his convention's audience were the only votes he and his party cared about.

The weekend before the election I got to see firsthand how the Romney campaign was only reaching out to their target voters when I was in Wisconsin, an important swing state. Obama's momentum was building in Wisconsin, too.

I held a GOProud get-together and did some interviews with local media. I also planned to do some volunteering for the Romney campaign. It was a good state for me to be in, because there was also an important Senate race there in which we had endorsed former Governor Tommy Thompson in his campaign against openly gay Congresswoman Tammy Baldwin. Baldwin ended up winning, but I was okay with that. The historical significance of electing the first openly gay person to the US Senate was certainly not lost on me. It was a good thing.

I checked into my hotel in downtown Milwaukee and learned that Romney campaign staffers had just checked out. Even though I had told Joshua and Katie that I would be in Wisconsin, neither bothered to mention that I could have attended a rally outside of Milwaukee that day. I held the GOProud get-together that evening, but I didn't end up doing anything with the Romney campaign, in part because their operations were set up in the suburbs, where all GOP operations are generally set up. I liked to do GOProud events downtown in cities because that's where the gays are used to going. Like many in Romney's 47 percent, the gays are often urban dwellers.

Being downtown in several big and midsized cities that fall, I was able to see and feel the anti-Romney, pro-Obama momentum building among voters there. Just to state a fact, more people live in urban areas than rural areas, and elections are won by the person who gets the most votes. I knew Romney would lose because I was in the places where the people were, and most of them weren't for him. I guessed that most of my Republican friends had spent most of their time that campaign season in Republican-leaning ex-urban and rural America, and that's where they got the impression everyone loved Romney. (The problem for them in the future is that ex-urban and rural America is becoming more multicultural too.)

The next morning I saw more evidence of Obama's momentum. One of the longest lines I've ever seen wrapped around the hotel and through the streets of downtown Milwaukee. The streets were blocked off and there were Secret Service agents in the hotel lobby. The president was about to appear at a rally at the convention center that was connected to the hotel. I decided that since the streets were blocked and I couldn't get the rental car out of the garage to get to the outskirts of town to Romney's office to make phone calls like I had sort of planned, that I would just have breakfast there and work in the lobby before my flight back to DC that afternoon.

It wasn't long before there was a lot of commotion in the hotel lobby. Living in Washington, I was familiar with the scene that was caused when a president arrives, so I was sure that's what was happening. Nope, I was wrong. It was pop star Katy Perry on her way to sing at the Obama rally. She created as much, if not more, commotion than a president.

The crowds outside the convention center were growing. They were standing in line for hours in the freezing cold, and it was snowing. That's what happens when you connect with people and convince them that you care about them—even when you have a disastrous economic record. People were willing to freeze their asses off just to get a chance to see him. It appeared to me that the cultural assault on Romney and the Republicans, waged by the Obama campaign, had worked.

10

THE VOTE

It had been a long year, but we finally reached the end of the 2012 presidential campaign. It was Election Day, the time for all Americans to come together to do our solemn duty in the voting booth.

Since moving to Washington, I had lived in several places, all in the Capitol Hill neighborhood. For the longest time I didn't change my voter registration address from my first place near the Capitol because that precinct has the coolest polling place location in the whole country. It's just a block and a half from the Capitol on East Capitol Street, which is the road that runs perpendicular to the East Front of the Capitol. I loved voting there in the shadow of the Capitol.

Walking up Capitol Hill, contemplating one of our most solemn duties as citizens—the vote for president of the United States—I was conflicted. The leaves were starting to fall and they were crunching under my feet on the brick sidewalk. I wasn't sure what I would do when I got to the polling place. I began to replay all of my experiences with Mitt Romney over the course of the last five years. From the time we ran ads against him in 2008 while I was at Log Cabin to just a few days before when I was on television in Wisconsin as an advocate in support of his candidacy.

I didn't think that I had it in me to actually vote for him. I knew that I couldn't vote for President Obama. Most Americans aren't single-issue voters. Obama's support for marriage equality wasn't enough for me to ignore his failed economic record and our different views on so many other issues. Obama's vision of government and mine were just too far apart for me to cast my vote for him.

I had been a conservative Republican team player my whole life, but in that moment I realized that I couldn't do what I had always done before, fall in line and vote for our team's candidate. I wasn't willing to compromise my integrity by casting my vote for someone I found unacceptable. In that moment of clarity, I remembered that the act of voting is the most powerful individual political action each of us participates in. The act of voting is not a team activity.

★

I decided in the voting booth to vote for someone who demonstrated more common decency and genuineness than any other candidate I had encountered over the last two years. He was the person who actually demonstrated that he respected and cared about all Americans as equal individuals. He was also the candidate whom I agreed with on most issues. I voted for the Libertarian Party candidate, former New Mexico Governor Gary Johnson, for president of the United States. I knew he wouldn't win, but I was able to walk out of the polling place with a clear conscience. I knew that this time doing the right thing was more important than being a team player. I just couldn't vote for a man who lacked the ability to empathize with people who weren't like him. That is the most important characteristic in a president, and Mitt Romney didn't have it.

I had always prided myself on having the courage to be myself and to be authentic in my work in politics, even when it went against the grain. I was an outspoken gay conservative, after all. That taste of independence I experienced with my vote showed me that, even though I had never done anything I was opposed to in my effort to be a part of the team, I had compromised myself when I supported the "lesser of two evils candidates" with whom I had major disagreements. My vote that day was my first experience of 100 percent true authenticity in politics. That action, taken in the privacy of the voting booth, was the most significant thing I had ever done in politics. I resolved then that I would not give up my newfound authenticity to be a team player again.

It would still be a long road before I gave up on the Republican Party to become politically independent, but in hindsight, it is interesting that I found good a candidate in someone who had left the Republican Party. Johnson's courage to leave the party to stand up for what he believed in and have his voice heard in the political process was commendable. That takes guts.

Governor Johnson is not the only former Republican who should be celebrated for standing up for what he believes in, even when it's unpopular. Many have done it quietly and publicly. The first openly gay elected official in America was Harvey Milk, a member of the San Francisco Board of Supervisors who was elected as a Democrat in 1978. He had been a Republican prior to 1972. Think about the courage it took for him, an openly gay man, to stand up and put himself out there to run for public office way back in the 1970s. Gays had even less chance of being taken seriously back then. He gave a famous speech about gay rights in 1978 that has inspired many Americans. Milk spoke of the importance of standing up and being an example for others. He said in that speech, "You have got to give them hope." All of us should remember those words when we have opportunities to be leaders for others.

★

After I had cast my vote for Johnson, I decided to skip the RNC's "victory" party and stayed in the office to watch the returns. We had some refreshments and invited folks to hang out with us. I felt better than I had felt in months. A weight had been lifted from my shoulders.

As the results came in from across the country, I actually got tickled watching people like Karl Rove go apeshit on television in total disbelief that Romney was losing. I had a severe case of the told-ya-so's. I also sat there in disbelief at the fact that so many Republicans were so out of touch that they thought he would actually win. The fact that so many Republicans couldn't believe that Romney lost showed me that they truly lacked the ability to see why he would have been unacceptable to the majority of Americans.

Would those dedicated Republicans ever understand the damage that the coalition with the crazies did to their electability? Even though the problems in the party seemed insurmountable, I was still hopeful that the GOP would use this as the wake-up call the party needed. The party had no choice but to change, and I was still committed to making that happen. I had given too much of my pride to the party to give up now.

11

THE AUTOPSY

After the election, the Republican Party was reeling. It seemed that nobody on our side could believe that President Obama had won reelection. Well, believe it.

I found myself lying on another beach contemplating my future—again. A friend had invited me to spend Thanksgiving with him in Cabo San Lucas, Mexico. That was just what I needed after the wringer I had been put through as the gay for Romney. One day we drove up the Pacific coast to find a remote beach that was home to a small surfing community. I lay there in the sand wondering if I could make a living if I opened a little taco stand on that beach. Selling tacos to surfers sounded so much better than returning to Washington to get back into the fray. I also wondered if the GOP had gotten the wake-up call they needed.

In the aftermath of the Romney defeat, there were lots of news stories and commentary that indicated to me that Republicans were starting to understand that the party wasn't demonstrating a modern cultural view. As many reflected on the election loss, it appeared that more and more influencers were beginning to comprehend that the GOP was failing to show empathy with voters and to connect on a cultural level. I was especially encouraged to read about the planned Republican National Committee review, infamously called "The Autopsy." Finally, they seemed to understand that there were fundamental problems in how the party was adapting to the changing multicultural landscape.

There was a series of conference calls with Republican leaders led by the team of high-profile consultants conducting the Autopsy. I was a part of a couple of those calls. After one of them, in which I clearly demonstrated that I got it, I received an email from former Bush White House press secretary and communications consultant Ari Fleischer, one of the project's leaders, requesting a one-on-one call. I thought that maybe they would finally listen to me. We spoke on the phone for about an hour a few days later.

Ari got an earful from me that day. I told him my whole story about my experience with the Romney campaign and about all the good talk, but no real action, on the part of Reince Priebus and the RNC. He stopped me at one point and said, "Good God, man! Why have you stayed a Republican?" I told him that I have stayed because I didn't have anywhere to go, and honestly, I felt that it was important for gay people to be represented among Republicans. Mitt Romney might have won, and it was important that I stayed, just in case he had been elected president. Ari knew the problems regarding the party's relationship with gay people, but I don't think he had ever realized how those problems manifested themselves.

In the months since I've left the party, I've often wondered why Ari and those who knew my story have stayed. I believe they have stayed because too many straight, white Republicans lack the ability to truly empathize with others who aren't like them. It was horrible that it happened to me, but it didn't happen to them or people like them, so it was okay with them. At least that's how I see it, from my perspective. Perception is reality in politics.

I told Ari that there is a reason that many Americans think that the GOP doesn't like them. It's not just lack of outreach, it's open hostility. I know that immigrants and other groups have experienced that too. I also told him that you can't pick and choose which groups to try to make amends to. Anyone who has ever been treated differently has a sense of solidarity with others who experience different treatment, whatever the reasons. If the party is hostile to one group or multiple groups of Americans, then all Americans are turned off. If you don't make it right with everyone, then you might as well stay an old, straight, white party.

I was hopeful after my conversation with Ari that the Republican National Committee would take the necessary steps to become a modern national party. I thought there was a chance that they would make bold moves, similar to what the Tories did in the United Kingdom, to show that they were in touch with real life today. David Cameron won election as prime minister in the UK by totally rebranding the Conservative Party. In addition to other bold rebranding moves, he showed that Conservatives cared about environmental and climate issues and aggressively moved the party to modernize on issues affecting gay people. He made concrete policy decisions, including supporting marriage equality, as well as political efforts that included aggressive outreach to the gay community in his campaigns. On the environment, the Conservatives went so far to demonstrate their commitment to pro-environment policies as to change their party's logo to a tree! Cameron was able to make such bold moves because he didn't have to contend with as large of a socially conservative constituency in his country. His rebranding efforts worked. He's still in office today, having won reelection in 2015. *Maybe*, I thought, *Republicans would make similar bold moves.*

There were several other conference calls and one-on-one calls I had around that time with prominent Republicans who were committed to righting the ship, so to speak. I was starting to get upbeat and a little excited for the future. There was a glimmer of hope again. Maybe this was the time to actually make it all happen. *Stay focused*, I thought to myself, *now is my time to lead. Finally, this is my chance. They are ready to listen this time.*

It was March 2013, and it was time for CPAC again. For the second year, GOProud was banned from sponsorship. Several of our friends worked to try to change that situation, but it was the way it was—as long as Cardenas was in charge at the ACU, there would be no GOProud. Honestly, that didn't change in 2014 when Cardenas left the ACU. Under new chairman Matt Schlapp, a disciple of Bush's 2004 architect Karl Rove, the ACU continues to exclude gay groups from sponsorship.

In 2013, the folks at the Competitive Enterprise Institute, a think tank with a libertarian bent, organized an event in the CPAC host hotel and, as a CPAC sponsor, they were able to get it listed on the CPAC schedule. Their program was called "A Rainbow on the Right: Growing the Coalition, Bringing Tolerance Out of the Closet." It was a panel discussion and I was asked to be a part of it.

This was my chance to have the last word about CPAC and, more importantly, deliver a message about the future of the conservative movement. Chris told me later that he would have loved the opportunity to do that. I didn't blame him for feeling that way. By that point, though, he had pretty much checked out of GOProud. He hadn't been into the office since election night and it was clear he had one foot out the door. With all of the setbacks over the last couple of years, it just wasn't as much fun around GOProud anymore, and besides, he had a lot of work to do with his consulting clients.

Most of the time when I give speeches, I write out a page or two of talking points or just a general outline. I knew that my remarks at CPAC would be widely reported. I knew what was riding on that speech, so I wrote it out word for word and practiced it.

The program was in the evening, but I had told ACU board member Suhail Khan that I would stop by another "inclusion" meeting and say a few words earlier that afternoon. I also had some media interviews lined up at the hotel. Around noon, I put on my favorite blue suit and red tie and got ready for my big day. I looked good, and felt good getting out of the car at the conference. I know it sounds silly, but that little thing really boosted my confidence as I entered the lion's den.

I walked into the lobby and heads started turning. It seemed like everyone knew who I was. The gay had arrived. There were college kids coming up to me and asking to take their photo with me, and some wanted my autograph on their conference programs. I moved through the hotel lobby with a bit of a crowd following me at first.

A professional photographer had asked to photograph me with his antique camera when I arrived, so I made my way through the conference hotel to find him. He ended up on the other side of the "radio row" area, so I stopped along the way and talked to hosts and friends gathered in that area. I found the photographer and we got ready for a short photo shoot. His antique camera was the type that you have to stand very, very still for. As I stood there, very still, a few people started to gather around to watch him take my picture. That was when I started to get nervous about the program we were doing later. The attention I attracted when I arrived, and now with the onlookers watching me have my picture taken, made it clear that our panel discussion about inclusion was going to be the highlight of the day at CPAC.

This time, I was the messenger. This time it was my voice, a gay conservative delivering the message to the conservative movement. We weren't relying on our straight conservative allies. It was also the first time that I really realized the power of my own voice, and the power of the platform we had built with GOProud.

The young people wanted their photo with me. People noticed me walk through the lobby. Radio hosts mentioned on air to their audiences that I was walking past as they described the scene at CPAC. That was all evidence to me that we had built a solid brand and that I had a voice. Now it was time to use it.

The Log Cabin Republicans had hired a new executive director and he was there in the audience at our program. I was milling around before our panel started and I said to him, "Well, I'm either going to drop a bomb or lay an egg with this speech. I'm just going to let it loose, we'll see how it lands." Then he said something to me that was very conventional, safe, and Log Cabin-ish. "Why don't you just want to have a nice panel? Why does it always have to be 'go big' with you?"

"Because changing the world and making history is big," I said. If you stay inside the box, always playing by the established rules, then change will never happen. It was time for change.

Our panel was moderated by Competitive Enterprise Institute's founder Fred Smith, and the panelists included *National*

Review's Jonah Goldberg, *Washington Post*'s Jen Rubin, Liz Mair, Margaret Hoover, and me. I had requested to be the first speaker on the panel because I didn't want to feel I had to respond to what anyone else said in their opening remarks. I wanted to set the tone for the evening.

The room was absolutely packed. There were people sitting on the floor, in the aisles, and standing wherever they could. It was so packed that they were turning people away because of the fire code. I looked out at the crowd and saw a lot of good conservative friends had shown up to support us. I also saw a few liberal gay reporters. One of them, Michelangelo Signorile, had often been a critic of GOProud and our efforts. I was glad that he and the others were there to see the outpouring of support we were receiving from the right, and to see how we were changing its atmosphere to be more welcoming of LGBT people. Critics on both sides saw the impact our work had on the conservative movement.

Just before I went to take my place at the front of the room, David Keene and his wife, Donna, came in. I took one look at him and my eyes welled up with tears. He and I had been through the war together and it meant the world to me to see him there on the night when I got to have the last word in that fight. He came over and shook my hand and gave me a hug. He told me that he and Donna couldn't stay, but he wanted to make sure everyone saw him there supporting us. He wasn't the chairman of the ACU's board anymore. He was the new president of the National Rifle Association's board. (That's a much bigger deal.) David knew how important it was for the conservative movement to include gay conservatives, and he again demonstrated it with that hug that night.

David and others like me in the movement knew that culture was moving, and conservatives needed to catch up. I wasn't going to let my experience with CPAC and the Romney campaign take my focus off our broader goals. Now was the time to be direct and to the point, because time was running out for them. America had moved forward, and conservatives were still too far back in the past.

It was time to start the program, so I moved to the front of the room and Fred stepped to the podium to introduce me. I was nervous, but the crowd was in my corner, so that helped to calm the nerves. I gave the speech I had come to deliver. I gave them my prescription for the conservative movement and Republican Party to evolve culturally. I called for a total recalibration of the conservative movement and talked about ways to grow the movement to build a new modern coalition that could win national elections.

Many thought I would come to that event with a conciliatory tone in an effort to try to get back into CPAC. I didn't do that. I was optimistic and hopeful for the future of the conservative movement, but I was also frank about the tolerance of bigotry in the movement. Conservatives needed to hear, in no uncertain terms, that bigotry stains everyone if it's tolerated. That's why it has to be called out and denounced. It's not okay to ignore it anymore.

I have never thought that those who oppose gay marriage are automatically anti-gay bigots. Anyone who at one time or another has opposed gay marriage is not necessarily a homophobe. It takes some people longer to come around to the position of support than others.

It is important in politics to be very cognizant of where the country's cultural evolution is at any given moment. That's especially true, in recent years, regarding gay marriage and gay people in general. Public opinion has moved farther and faster on gay marriage than on any other cultural issue. In fact, by 2013, GOProud had officially expanded our mission to include working on state issues such as marriage. Given where the country was at that moment, it was time to push the right harder than we had done before. It wouldn't be long before the only people who were left opposing marriage equality would be the bigots.

★

Including bigots in the coalition would do catastrophic damage to the conservative movement and the Republican Party. There aren't very many voters in America who base their votes on the specific issue of legal civil marriage for gay couples, but attitudes toward that issue and homosexuality in general are a key cultural indicator for many voters to determine if a candidate or party sees things the way they do. It was time for the right to evolve already.

The news reports the next day were amazing. What I didn't know then was that just before our panel, there was an anti-gay panel that took place in a virtually empty room. Cleta Mitchell was on that panel. Chris Geidner, who was by then a reporter with Buzzfeed, ran an image with a photo of our packed, standing-room-only program next to a picture of Cleta's empty room. His story and that image went viral on the Internet. It was everywhere the next day with the headline, "At CPAC, The Marriage Fight Is Over."

★

It was. In fact, by then, the marriage debate was effectively over everywhere in America, not just at CPAC. Public opinion polls consistently showed the majority of Americans supporting marriage equality, and in the 2012 elections, just a few months before, voters in four states had voted down anti-gay ballot measures and voted in support of civil marriage for gay couples. That was the first time that had ever happened. The gays had won the debate.

Republican US Senator Rob Portman (R-OH) announced his support for marriage equality that same weekend, and the issue gained even more momentum on the right. I was on television and all over the Internet as the "gay marriage guy" on the right. A lot of gay liberals cried foul because they felt that GOProud hadn't previously made marriage a priority and that I was late to the party on that issue. Again, they didn't understand our strategy or the fact that they were never our audience. We always delivered the message that our audience in the conservative movement needed to hear, when they were ready to hear it. Senator Portman helped to open up a more direct dialogue on the issue. He did it when we did it, likely for the same reason. It was after the election, and we were all done being anti-gay marriage Mitt Romney's team players.

Had Portman or GOProud been beating the marriage drum the summer before, we would have been seen just how organizations such as Conservatives for the Freedom to Marry and Log Cabin are seen by grassroots conservatives. Conservatives view them as liberal Republicans who aren't team players. Their messengers didn't carry the weight with the conservative audience that ours did. We were team players when we had to be, and advocates for change when the time was right. That timing was based on where the country and, more importantly, our conservative audience were in their evolutions.

The Autopsy report came out and called for aggressive outreach to diverse communities. I was encouraged. On the other hand, I was disappointed because it didn't call for outreach directly to the gay community, like it did for other demographic groups. It was, however, the first-ever RNC document to use the word "gay" in a non-negative context.

The Autopsy mentioned that younger voters care about issues affecting their gay friends and family. The statement didn't go far enough, but baby steps were positive, even if the "baby" taking them should have been well past the point of walking. The country had moved beyond where the RNC thought it was. There was still too much deference to the bigots. Again, everyone has to be included or don't bother to expand your brand, because what will be remembered is the exclusion of some. The report stopped short of calling for real modernization for fear of pissing off the crazies.

The baby steps at rebranding the Republican Party were a good start, but how did it plan to attract normal people and independents into its ranks? The report called for outreach to diverse demographic groups, but with the exception of stating that, the party's position on immigration turned off voters. There was very little discussion of changing the message that would be delivered in their outreach efforts.

The problems with the party were more extensive than just that diverse communities weren't hearing their message. The Autopsy report ignored many of those problems.

There were soon plenty of examples of the prominent presence of the intolerant wing of the GOP. Just as the RNC was trying to set their half-assed rebranding effort in motion, one of its members, Dave Agema from Michigan, gave an interview while at the RNC's spring meeting in which he said that gays should get into treatment for their homosexuality.

This wasn't the first time Agema had beaten the anti-gay drum, but this time he was shitting all over the RNC's new,·

kinder, gentler tone. He had been on GOProud's radar as one
of the most anti-gay voices on the 163-member Republican
National Committee for a long time. He wasn't the only one, of
course, but with these remarks, he seemed intent on poking his
finger in the eye of Chairman Reince Priebus and the Autopsy
report. I blasted him in the press a bit, and I reached out behind
the scenes to Priebus's office.

I scheduled a meeting with RNC deputy chief of staff Sara
Armstrong. I remember walking across Capitol Hill over to the
RNC office. It was Good Friday, a warm sunny day, and Washington felt like a ghost town as families fled town to make an
early exit for spring break. I thought about wearing jeans to the
meeting, but that would be too casual for the RNC office even
on a holiday Friday, so I wore dark slacks and a nice shirt.

When I got to the RNC's offices on the House side of the
Hill, I was met by a young intern who escorted me up to the
fourth floor, where the chairman's and the executive staff offices
are. The young man was dressed in a full suit, complete with
his American flag and RNC lapel pins. I looked at him and
asked why he was so dressed up on a Friday before a holiday.
He replied that it was a professional look and that he liked it. I
looked him dead in the eye and said, "And they say the RNC is
out of touch." Then I gave him a condescending grin.

I sat down with Sara in a conference room. We chatted about
Agema, and she said that it was the RNC's position that there was
really nothing they could do to sanction him or even shut him
up. I said that he was doing great damage to the party, and she
agreed with me. I told her that the chairman should denounce
him. Priebus only went so far as to say that everyone should be
treated with "dignity and respect." Rank bigotry didn't deserve
dignity and respect. It should be called out and condemned.

Then I took the opportunity to use this as my last-ditch effort to make my case for modernization of the party directly to a decision maker. "It is time to actually do something, instead of just talking about it," I told her, "to show that Republicans don't hate gay people." She praised our work and said we'd been doing a great job to show that. I explained that every time we reached out to establishment Republican leaders, including that office, for support in our efforts, we had been met with a face palm. "I am tired of building one-way bridges," I said. She knew I was right, and she acknowledged that there was not much that could be done about it because of the fear of backlash from the anti-gay industry.

I brought up other ways the GOP appears out of touch with modern life in America, other than the gay stuff. Some of it was purely superficial and cosmetic, and easier to fix than the real problems. I pointed out the bookcases with porcelain elephants and Abraham Lincoln busts that they used for background in their videos. It looked so old-fashioned and stuck in the past. I suggested that they do more casual "Oprah-style" videos and programs, and less of a suited-up chairman speaking behind a podium with a GOP seal on it. I even suggested changing the culture in the office. "Why is a twenty-two-year-old intern wearing a suit on a holiday Friday?" I asked matter-of-factly.

"The chairman wears a suit every single day," she said. "He has done away with the previous chairman's policy that allows the staff to wear jeans on Fridays."

The problem at the RNC was clear. There was an out-of-touch, lapel-pin-wearing, suburban-dwelling douchebag at the top of the RNC's food chain. The RNC's problem rested with Priebus himself.

Priebus had told Chris and me a year before that he wasn't able to do any public engagement with the gay community because he'd "get a call from [the Family Research Council's] Tony Perkins." Since a call from Perkins was to be avoided, I tried to think of steps they could take that wouldn't cause backlash. I suggested that the RNC hire a gay person as their new urban outreach director. They already had a department for outreach to black voters, and gays and blacks make up some of the largest demographic groups in most urban areas, so that made sense since they couldn't or wouldn't hire any LGBT outreach staff. The Democrats have had an LGBT director since the Clinton years.

I still wanted Republicans to succeed, even though I felt that I was grasping at straws trying to think of anything palatable for them to do that would be proactive. I left that meeting having gotten a bunch off my chest, but with zero confidence that anything would ever change; Priebus and the others lacked the backbone to stand up to the crazies. My nickname for Priebus is "Pussy Galore." It just seems to fit him.

By this point, GOProud was running out of money and I didn't have it in my heart anymore to get out there and try to fund-raise. It was too hard to make a case for it anymore.

Chris and I did an interview with Chris Geidner to announce that we were both leaving the day-to-day management of the organization, but would remain on the board of directors of the organization we founded. I was hoping for the best for GOProud, but honestly, I didn't really care what happened to it. It would have been okay with me if it just shut down.

I ended up leaving the board soon after that, and GOProud did eventually close its doors a little over a year after Chris and I left. There wasn't enough support for the organization from gay or straight conservatives. Besides, the conservative movement and the Republican Party had made it perfectly clear that there wasn't a place for gays on their team. The Log Cabin group still technically exists, but it's barely a shell of what it was before 2008.

I began to plan my next steps. In other words, I really needed a job.

I did get a consulting contract to work with the American Civil Liberties Union's (ACLU) Out for Freedom campaign to work to expand civil marriage for gay couples to all fifty states. The ACLU was attacked, publicly and privately, by liberal gay activists and organizations when it was announced that they had hired me. The left objected to my being brought into their coalition. I was surprised at that, because now I was working on a single issue that we all agreed on. That wasn't enough for the all-or-nothing gay left. I was sidelined there, and my contract with the ACLU only lasted three months.

I was working for the ACLU—in fact, it was my first day there—on the day the US Supreme Court issued their decision that struck down the Defense of Marriage Act (DOMA), though. That was an amazing day. I walked over to the SCOTUS in the morning. I had a documentary filmmaker following me around because she was doing a video profile of me. I ran into Michelangelo Signorile, and he interviewed me for his radio show. That was the first time he actually saw me as a caring individual, instead of some hard-hearted right-winger. I got a little choked up during the interview when I was describing the historic scene in front of the Court. I remember standing there at the bottom of the Supreme Court's steps next to Democratic Congresswoman Jan Jakowski when the decisions came down. There were lots of Democratic members of Congress there, but I didn't see any Republican members there to witness history. The gays won. DOMA was found to be unconstitutional.

12

NO HOPE

As I began to distance myself more and more from GOProud and shed my skin as the head of the team-player conservative gays, I started to look at things with a little more of an impartial eye. Despite all of our victories to expand the inclusiveness of gay people on the right, the anti-gay forces weren't dissolving like I had thought they would. To be sure, pro-gay voices now had a place in the conservative movement, thanks to our hard work, but anti-gay voices still wielded too much power.

One of the biggest signs that the new, post-Autopsy GOP was still hopelessly out of touch was the race for Governor of Virginia. The Republicans nominated anti-gay homophobe Ken Cuccinelli, the Virginia Attorney General. I couldn't understand why my friends in the GOP and my Tea Party friends were so excited about him. He was waaay outside the mainstream on a number of cultural issues. On abortion, Cuccinelli was a chief proponent of the controversial proposed law that would have required women to have a "transvaginal" ultrasound prior to having an abortion. On gays, he has said that we are "soulless" and "in need of help," among many, many other crazy things.

His positions and rhetoric on education, immigration, and other cultural issues didn't seem based in reality either.

It was shocking to me that the Republican Party thought that Cuccinelli was an acceptable candidate. This guy was as crazy a gubernatorial nominee as we've seen since Republicans in Louisiana nominated racist David Duke, a former Ku Klux Klan leader, in the early 1990s. Back then, Duke was running against ethically challenged Edwin Edwards. The legendary political bumper sticker VOTE FOR THE CROOK, IT'S IMPORTANT was created in that race.

Cuccinelli was running against an ethically challenged Democrat, former Clinton crony Terry McAuliffe. I incurred the wrath of activists on the right when I publicly compared the Cuccinelli-McAuliffe race to the Duke-Edwards race. FOX News commentator Erick Erickson blasted me on his popular blog RedState, and said that Chris and I (and GOProud) were never really committed conservatives anyway. Of course I was a conservative, but I wasn't going to be associated with bigotry any longer. Erickson and others didn't recognize that there comes a point in society's cultural maturity when old, traditional points of view begin to be unacceptable. Candidates and parties become undesirable, regardless of their good positions on other things, such as taxes. In other words, a bigot with a good tax plan is still a bigot, and an unacceptable candidate. The voters of Virginia knew that, and they ended up electing the ethically challenged McAuliffe.

On election night, 2013, I went to New Jersey to celebrate Governor Chris Christie's reelection victory. It was truly a scene that I had wanted to see for years at a Republican event. Christie's victory party was diverse, reflecting the modern diversity of the state and, frankly, our country. There were black people, Hispanic people, women, and gays, and they weren't just tokens brought in to help the optics. They were genuine fans of Governor Christie, because Christie has the natural ability to show genuine empathy and he's able to demonstrate that he can see things from others' perspectives, even if he hasn't always shown it.

On my way to the party I rode the elevator with New Mexico Governor Susanna Martinez and her husband. She had been on the campaign trail with Christie over the last couple of days of the campaign. She wowed the inner-city crowds in Newark and other stops in New Jersey with her personable demeanor and her ability to communicate with Hispanic voters in Spanish. I thought that the Christie-Martinez campaign stops looked like a very good potential 2016 national ticket. They had great chemistry together, and they really connected with crowds. I doubted if the GOP would be that smart to nominate them though. Both Christie and Martinez have gone off the conservative reservation on a couple issues, which would turn off the all-or-nothing crowd on the right. Christie has also had ethical issues since then that may prevent him from achieving higher office.

At the end of the night, I ended up on that same elevator with Reince Priebus. He and I shared relief that a really crazy bigot had lost a special election for Congress in Alabama that night. I also told him that I knew that he would get criticism for not doing more to help Cuccinelli in Virginia, because it turned out to be a closer race than anyone was expecting, but he should know that he dodged a bullet. Had Cuccinelli been elected, the GOP would have the Governor of Virginia, one of the most high-profile governors in the country, making comments and pushing policies that would seriously hamper Reince's efforts to grow the party, even though I thought Reince's efforts didn't scratch the surface of what needed to be done.

So I left New Jersey that night with mixed feelings. On one hand, Governor Christie was showing that it was possible for Republicans to run a culturally connected, winning campaign, but on the other there was Virginia and Alabama. Christie didn't have to contend with very many of the culturally out-of-touch social conservatives in New Jersey the way the GOP had to do on the national level. They were still a big force in the national Republican Party, and they weren't going anywhere.

Over the years, I have heard from gay people all over the world who have admired what we did with GOProud. I've especially made friends with several right-of-center gays from Australia. In fact, one prominent gay conservative there, Australian Human Rights Commissioner Tim Wilson, and I had at one time discussed the possibility of organizing an international conference of free-market, freedom-loving gays. That never came about, but many gay people from places such as Bolivia, Ghana, Chile, Spain, Serbia, Germany, Canada, and many other countries have reached out to me over the years.

They contact me in part for camaraderie with other people like them who think like them. We share the understanding that limited-government, free-market policies are good for our global economy, because less government intervention in commerce and trade makes markets available to everyone around the world. We also know that promoting freedom shouldn't end at our borders, and we stand in solidarity in support for liberty and freedom for everyone in all corners of the world, including all gay people in the world.

In fact, gays in Canada and Australia have started groups in their countries that were directly inspired by our success with

GOProud. One of the Australian organizers, Matthew Lesh, was visiting Washington, and asked me if I would take him and a friend to Grover's Wednesday Meeting. I hadn't been to the meeting in a couple of months, because I had not felt much like a team player anymore, but I said I would take them. Besides, I thought it would be good to see what everyone was up to.

It was a really cold January day in 2014. Honestly, I couldn't understand why Matthew had chosen that time of year to come to the US, but he was in DC and I was taking him to the meeting. We showed up, and there at the table next to Grover was Cleta Mitchell. I pulled Matthew and his friend aside and told them who Cleta was. They were intrigued at the inside scoop about one of Washington's most notorious anti-gay operators.

Cleta was there to talk about some of the work she was doing relating to the Internal Revenue Service (IRS) and the way the IRS appeared to be going after organizations who were organized under section 501c4 of the tax code. The IRS was targeting c4's based on their political activity. She was working to fight some of the proposed new IRS regulations that organizations, both on the right and the left, opposed. Honestly, there is probably nobody in politics in Washington who disagreed with her on that issue. Many people in the room, including some who were very supportive of GOProud and gay conservatives, were lavishing praise on her for her anti-IRS work. The culture regarding homosexuality had moved so far, so fast, that it rendered Cleta's point of view unacceptable in 2014. No matter how great her other work might have been, her bigotry should have made her too toxic to be presenting at the Wednesday Meeting.

I reflected on some of our tactics and strategies over the years. When we were saying that it was okay to work with people who disagreed with us on the issue of marriage, did people think we were saying to tolerate anti-gay homophobes too? Didn't they get it? Didn't they understand that we wanted to marginalize the bigots? Our goal wasn't to end up with a coalition of both modern thinkers and out-of-touch bigots. Legitimizing the unacceptable views-of-the past by keeping them as part of the team wasn't okay anymore. The display at Grover's that day showed me that no matter how many of them wanted gays in the movement, they still wanted to keep one foot in the past by tolerating what was now unacceptable to the rest of America.

I haven't been back to the Wednesday Meeting since that day, and I haven't been a Republican since then, either. That was the day before my swim when I decided to change my party registration. That was the moment when my hope had run out. That was the straw on the camel's back that finally broke my will to continue the fight to help them. How could I help people who tolerated rank bigotry? Besides, what was the use? If the purpose was to win elections, how could the Republicans win a national election again if they included and tolerated bigots in their coalition? Sure, they may win in regions that favor their rural white demographic base, but winning a national election again in a country as diverse as we are now is a different thing. The rapidly changing multicultural demographics in suburban and rural America would diminish their regional strength eventually, too.

Not only was trying to help them change a waste of time, but there comes a time in every failed noble effort when those who tried but failed begin to look out of touch with reality if they continue their futile work. I knew that if I continued my work to help modernize the GOP, then I would look like I was ignorant of reality too. I would end up appearing no better than the worst of them. I didn't want to waste my time in a hopeless effort that would soon have a negative effect on me and my character. I continue to hope that my friends in the conservative movement and Republican Party will come to realize that too. I hate the fact that so many good people in the GOP look no better than the bigots they tolerate.

Things haven't gotten any better in the GOP since I left. In fact, in many ways it's worse.

Very soon after I left the party, RNC member Dave Agema again had a couple of lovely episodes that got a lot of news coverage—and caused my blood to boil. First he said something egregious about gay people in a radio interview, then a day or two later he posted something truly unbelievable on Facebook. He said, among other things about Muslims, that no Muslim had done anything positive to help our country.

Priebus was silent. No reaction.

The timing of the Agema controversy fueled the media story about my leaving the Republican Party. It was an example that was delivered to me on a silver platter. I cited his views about gays and Muslims as unacceptable everywhere in America except the Republican National Committee. I told the gay magazine *The Advocate,* and restated on MSNBC, that Reince didn't have the balls to do what he should do to modernize the GOP. I know that got Priebus mad, or at least I hope it did. He deserved it. It was a few days after, when the story fueled by me wouldn't go away, that Reince finally called for Agema to resign. He didn't resign. He remained a member of the Republican National Committee.

Old habits die hard, and when the Agema story broke, I reached out to the RNC and warned Sara that this was a big story, and they should prepare to do damage control during their annual meeting that week in Washington. The theme of their meeting was inclusion and outreach. The Agema story and the story of my leaving the party totally trashed their intended message. The truth was more powerful than the RNC spin about their halfhearted attempts at inclusion.

The GOP continues to demonstrate their cultural disconnect. The new priority for the anti-gay industry is "religious freedom," a rebranded term for anti-gay discrimination. That has become the mantra of the anti-gay right. Now that they know that they've lost, they've decided to play the victim and demand that they have the "right," because of their religious beliefs, to discriminate against gay people. That's the same argument that has been used for millennia to push back against cultural evolution, but the reality is that many times throughout history, deeply held religious beliefs have changed and simply been proven to be wrong. That's certainly been the case with issues regarding gender and race, and now it's true for sexual orientation. Some religions today have evolved more than others in those areas. That's easy to see when you compare today's fundamentalist Muslims with modern liberal strains of Christianity.

In March 2015, the anti-gay right was met with that new modern reality in Indiana. The anti-gay lobbyists helped to usher a new law through the Indiana state legislature that included a provision that would have provided protections for those who discriminate in public accommodation and commerce based on their religious beliefs. Indiana Governor Mike Pence was a strong proponent of the bill, signed the bill into law, and then incurred the wrath of major international backlash, especially from the corporate world, where legalized discrimination of any kind should not be tolerated.

Major corporations such as Apple, SalesForce.com, Marriott, and others big name companies condemned the state's actions and called for the law's repeal. The mayor of Indianapolis, a Republican, called for the legislature to amend the state's civil rights law to include LGBT people, something that had never been done there before. The mayor and the corporate leaders understood the new modern reality because they operate in a diverse modern world.

Having worked in this arena for years, I had followed the career of Governor Pence for a long time. He was a former congressman from a rural Indiana district, largely made up of straight, white Christians, before being elected governor. He had always made his opposition to homosexuality a priority in his public life. I used to say that the first thing that Mike Pence must do when he wakes up in the morning is try to figure out how he can stick it to the gays today. This time, the country and world stuck it to him. The public relations hit he took effectively removed him from consideration of ever being on a national GOP ticket. Deservingly, his image was tarnished and his political career destroyed.

Governor Pence was forced to walk back his position and seek changes to the law, but that was after all the major 2016 presidential candidates had rushed to his defense voicing their support for the pro-discrimination law. They did that either because they truly supported it or to pander to those who do. Either way, it's unacceptable in today's America.

One of those candidates voicing his support for pro-discrimination laws was former Florida Governor Jeb Bush, the brother of former President George W. Bush. Jeb Bush had an ugly anti-gay record as governor, and now he wanted to get elected president. He was positioning himself as a moderate, reasonable alternative to some of the more conservative candidates in the race. It reminded me of his brother's "compassionate conservative" campaign in 2000. I decided, right then and there, that the Bush family wasn't going to have another opportunity to use gay Americans as a wedge to get the votes of bigots.

13

THE FOX NEWS BLOWTORCH

The media plays a big role in fanning the flames of the culture wars and dividing Americans politically. Many on the right and the left take their cues and talking points from biased media on both sides. The days of nonbiased informative news/talk programming are over.

I was sitting with a friend at a conservative media conference and we were going on and on about our frustration with cable television news programming. We were frustrated because most cable news programs feature people from the right and the left arguing with standard, predictable talking points. That's certainly the case with FOX News Channel, which presents a conservative perspective, and MSNBC, with a left-leaning point of view. Even CNN features Republicans and Democrats presenting their teams' talking points, rather than freethinkers having a thoughtful discussion about the issues of the day.

My friend leaned over to me to whisper in my ear so the other conservative conference attendees would not hear. "Do you listen to NPR?" she asked. I told her that I did.

"I love NPR," she whispered, "I always learn something that I didn't know before. I never learn anything new from FOX News!"

She wasn't alone. There are lots of right-of-center people who listen to NPR and other media outlets for news and information. Whenever I've been on NPR, I've gotten tons of calls and messages from folks all over the country who heard me on the radio. Most normal people get their news and information from a variety of sources, including the thoughtful, informative programming on NPR.

Unfortunately, not everyone is like that. Some people, especially on the right, consume news and commentary only from sources that they know present a point of view that they are likely to agree with. The fact that Republican politicians and their base of voters on the right are so out of touch is exacerbated by the conservative media that plays on their emotions and fears to drive ratings. I can't stand that so many activists on the right know that the anti-gay folks are wrong, yet tolerate them anyway. It simply disgusts me to see television executives pander to the crazies to drive ratings.

Over the years, I've had a lot of dealings with the most senior management at the most powerful conservative media outlet in the country, FOX News Channel. They are normal modern Americans who recognize the cultural evolution in America regarding homosexuality, yet they help to legitimize and propagate bigotry by continuing to put the voices of intolerance on their air. FOX does this as the top-rated cable news/talk channel on television, because their viewers are so loyal. According to a 2013 Gallup Poll, over 20 percent of Republicans report that FOX News Channel is their primary source of news and information, with CNN second at only 4 percent. All other news outlets were reported as the primary news source of 1 percent or less of Republicans. I know many Republicans who only watch FOX. That's why my friend whispered her question to me about listening to NPR, so that the other conservatives wouldn't know that she didn't only get her information from FOX!

One day in 2011, back when we were really rocking with GOProud, I was sitting at my desk in the office when my cell phone rang. "Hi Jimmy. This is Gina, from Roger Ailes's office. Roger was hoping that you would have time to come in and visit with him." Those were the words that almost every professional conservative activist would kill to hear. Roger, of course, was the founder and head of FOX News Channel and, frankly, the most influential conservative in America. I was on a train to New York City two days later for the big meeting.

"Jimmy, I've got a problem with the gay community," he said when I walked into his second-floor office at the News Corporation building on Sixth Avenue.

"No you don't," I said. "You have a problem with the gay left."

FOX had been the target of liberal groups such as Media Matters and GLAAD for their habit of giving prominent anti-gay spokespeople a platform on their air, and for rarely covering gay people in anything other than a negative light.

I knew going into the meeting that Roger Ailes, even more than Andrew Breitbart, lives in an "our side versus their side" world.

Roger was shorter than I expected. He was such a towering figure in the conservative world that I expected his physical stature to match. It didn't. He had a dozen or so televisions on the wall next to his desk. His shirt was rumpled, his tie loosened, and his collar unbuttoned. He wasn't wearing shoes and his socks were too big, leaving the toes of his tan-colored socks wrinkly and unfilled. We walked across his office to a sitting area. He sat in a chair across from me and put his socked feet up on a coffee table. Then he and I, along with his friend and lawyer Peter Johnson, Jr., engaged in an hour-long conversation about the FOX News Channel's coverage of the gay marriage issue and issues affecting gay people in general.

Roger told me that they can barely even mention gay marriage on the air, and certainly not in a positive way, without getting major blowback from the anti-gay segment of their audience. He also told me that they regularly hear from the anti-gay industry leaders like Tony Perkins about their coverage of gay issues. He said something like, "Look, I know where this issue is going to be in twenty years. We are going to look back in disbelief that there was ever a time when gays couldn't get married, but we aren't there yet. I'm just trying to figure out how to navigate this issue."

As one of the smartest strategists on the right and in television in general, Roger is keenly aware of where the country is at any given time. Through our conversation, I realized that he clearly understood that gay people are a part of normal life in America now, and he also knew that a segment of his audience is out of step with the majority of the American people. With that in mind, I essentially made our general GOProud pitch. I asked him to show how conservative policies benefit gay people too. I told him not to only mention gay people in the context of marriage, but also cover gay people just like every other group. I said that he should have openly gay people represented in their programming, too. I told him he could do that by putting me on television as a gay person advocating conservative positions on issues from taxes to regulation to foreign affairs. Put the gays on your side, Roger. The right has lost the culture war on homosexuality, so it's time to quit pretending that there is still a legitimate debate. Acknowledge that gays exist, put us on your side, and present our point of view.

One thing raised a red flag and showed me that while Roger understood the issue on an intellectual level, he wasn't exactly completely comfortable with gays. He knew the reality of where the country was heading, but he was a bit out of touch with that reality. He expressed concern about his son and what he would be taught about gay marriage in school. Really. He was actually concerned that his son might hear about gay people and the reality of gay marriage. That showed me that in his core he still wasn't any more comfortable with gays than many in his audience. He wanted to shield his son from the modern reality that gay people exist and get married nowadays. All I could think about at that moment was to wonder if Roger's son would turn out to be gay himself. I hoped so!

As a result of our meeting, I was back in New York a couple of weeks later to appear on a political panel on FOX's morning show *FOX and Friends*. I had been warned by friends that it was important at FOX to stick to the talking points that you provide the producers ahead of time or you may not get asked back. Well, doing that resulted in a just-okay performance. I was a little too stiff and not exactly answering the host's questions, because I stuck exactly to my prepared points. I did directly answer one of the host's questions off camera. Host Steve Doocy asked me what GOProud was. The other panelists, Democratic commentator Jehmu Greene and Congresswoman Marsh Blackburn (R-TN), both knew what GOProud was and both chimed in in positive ways when I answered him. Doocy did not react in a positive way. There's no other word to describe the look on his face than disgusted. He looked at me as if I had just punched a girl when he found out that GOProud was an organization for gay conservatives and their allies. I just wanted to shrivel up in the chair. I've been on that show several times since, but never again with Doocy. Every time I've appeared on that show since that day, I've been interviewed by the female cohost, Gretchen Carlson, then her replacement, Elisabeth Hasselbeck.

I got a boost of confidence when the panel was finished. Peter Johnson, Jr. was in the studio because he had brought his daughter to meet the guest that followed our panel, singer Selena Gomez. He made a point to come over to tell me that I did a good job. That helped me get back on my stride after Doocy threw me off. A few months later I went in to meet with Bill Shine, executive vice president of programming at both FOX News Channel and FOX Business Network. He is number two to Roger at both networks. Bill mentioned that he had heard about my appearance on *Fox and Friends*. He said in an exaggerated way, "Oh I heard about that." I didn't ask what he meant by that. I don't know if he got negative feedback from Doocy, the anti-gay industry, the audience, or all three.

In 2013 when the Supreme Court was hearing the oral arguments in the Windsor case regarding the Defense of Marriage Act (DOMA), I reached out to Shine to express my pleasure at the fact that they didn't have a bunch of the anti-gay folks, such as Tony Perkins and others, on their programs to rant about the societal evil of gay marriage. Bill said to me that they made the decision to have their reporters cover it and their anchors report on it, but they weren't going to put together panels to debate civil marriage for gay couples on their air, because, according to him, "the debate is over."

I loved hearing that, because of course it was true and it showed that FOX was making decisions to try to keep from showing conservatives on the wrong side of an issue that had been decided. That was a good thing for the team. Unfortunately, the anti-gay industry has found other ways to taint the conservative movement and the Republican Party on FOX News's programming. In fact, it's gotten much worse since that conversation with Shine.

It was later that year when something in the media showed the cultural disconnect on the right more than almost anything that I had ever been involved in: *Duck Dynasty*, a popular reality show on the A&E channel. It's a show about a family that romanticizes the lifestyle of stereotypical ignorant, backwoods rednecks. Even though a few of them are quite educated and successful businesspeople, they have made a fortune with a television show while playing the roles of rednecks. Video footage surfaced of the family patriarch, Phil Robertson, saying horribly homophobic things about gay people and also disturbing things about blacks being happier and better taken care of when they were on plantations during the era of slavery.

Phil Robertson's views about gay people and homosexuality reflect the most common and extreme form of religious-based bigotry. He cloaks his statements about gays in religion, but he says things that would make Jesus cry. Really extreme stuff.

There was a huge firestorm in the media about Robertson's statements and somehow it became a right-versus-left fight. Of course, the cable news networks, and especially FOX, were fanning the flames. Conservative pundits, even politicians such as Louisiana Governor Bobby Jindal and former vice-presidential nominee Sarah Palin, jumped to Robertson's defense. They were defending his right to free speech! Dammit!

I have done my share of defending people's right to be wrong. That's half of what we did at GOProud in order to build trust on the right, but where do you draw the line? Robertson's remarks were way over the line that any reasonable person should draw. Besides, there comes a point when if all you do is defend others' right to be wrong, then everyone is going to think that you are wrong too. That's especially true when you do it in the most extreme situations.

During that controversy, a political consultant friend from South Dakota reached out to me. He was friends with the Robertsons and was working with them to help manage the controversy. Phil's family knew that he was out of bounds and were afraid that the public-relations and economic consequences could be severe for their show and family business. They were seeking solutions to minimize the damage.

I think that nearly every gay group in the country reached out to the Robertsons in hopes of gaining access to their television audience. Most every group offered to do a "beer summit" type of public meeting with Phil, so that he could show that he was open to hearing a different point of view. I told my friend who was advising the family that I thought the engagement with gays should be more natural, and not as staged as a summit. A summit, or big formal meeting, would only continue to make the cultural controversy look political. I suggested that maybe the Robertsons "accidentally" end up in a gay bar and have a great time there, or maybe one of their hunting group friends comes out to Phil on camera. Make it natural and make it cultural, and part of the show, I advised.

At GOProud, we used to get a lot of complaints from some folks for hosting high-profile parties more often than we did policy-related panel discussions and "substantive things," as one critic said to me. Just like we did with the events with Ann Coulter and Andrew Breitbart, and the party at the convention, one thing I know is that a cultural message should be delivered in a cultural context, not a political one. That's why some of those parties were so successful for us—they demonstrated that there was a cultural shift on the right in the cultural context of a social event. When you are dealing with cultural issues, use culture to convey the message.

The Robertsons didn't take my advice, or anyone else's, for that matter. I think it was because Phil didn't want any part of appearing to evolve. In fact, he has since ramped up his anti-gay activism and he's paired it with conservative political activism. That's why it wasn't a surprise to me to see Phil receive a big award and give a speech, filled with offensive anti-gay pronouncements, on the main stage at CPAC in 2015. In the end, the Robertsons weathered the storm and lived to continue to offend polite society from sea to shining sea every week on their television show and with their activism.

It was around that time, both before and a little after, that I had some meetings in New York with executives at both MSNBC and FOX News in hopes of landing a paid political contributor contract to do television commentary. Honestly, I felt a little bit like Goldilocks, searching around trying to find a network that was "just right." The television executives all asked me, "Who are you going to be on our air?" I was still pitching myself as the gay Republican commentator, but that was getting harder to do because I would cringe every time I heard the word "Republican" attached to me. The people in those commentary jobs have to toe the party line for whichever team they're on when they are on the air. The executives at both networks made that clear. The problem was that I just wanted to go on television and say exactly what I thought about things.

I did get the opportunity to give my unfiltered point of view on television a couple of months later. There was a national controversy raging around the new CEO of the tech company Mozilla. Brendan Eich had been a financial supporter of the campaign to pass Proposition 8, just like San Diego hotel owner Doug Manchester had done, and the Mozilla board of directors was under fire for naming a Prop 8 supporter as its new CEO. Just as I thought that Manchester deserved the opportunity to redeem himself, I thought Eich deserved that chance too. Unfortunately, the board forced him to resign. I thought that both sides in this controversy, the activists who raised objections and the Mozilla board, were wrong. I had the opportunity to make my points in an interview with Elisabeth Hasselbeck on *FOX and Friends* one morning during the controversy.

Many on the right, including the cast of *FOX and Friends*, were defending Eich by making the point that President Obama had supported Prop 8 in 2008, too. They failed to recognize that Obama and most of America had evolved on that issue since then. Societal standards and norms had changed since 2008. I didn't think that it was fair that activists would attack Eich's actions in 2008 based on the cultural standards of 2014. I also said that gays won the culture war and we shouldn't seek retribution from our former opponents; we should just be grateful that future generations of gay Americans wouldn't have to deal with the institutional discrimination that we endured. In an "us versus them" world, both sides were mad at me now because I hadn't completely agreed with either of them.

That appearance set off a round of attacks on social media, especially from the right. Most notable was FOX News's religion editor Todd Starnes, who attacked and mocked me on Twitter. Starnes is FOX's resident anti-gay spokesperson, who is employed by FOX to promote many of the out-of-touch views of the social conservatives on their air. He was one of the top defenders of Eich's right to be wrong. He predictably challenged my assertion that society had evolved and that the gays had won.

There was a time, not that long before, when I would have carefully worded my statements on FOX so as not to offend social conservatives, but times had changed for me too. I was no longer trying to help them to evolve—I was now just telling it like it was. That pissed off Starnes and the fringe on the right, but it felt so good to do it! They needed a dose of reality served up to them on their home turf of FOX News.

It was only a few months later that I was in Bill Shine's office, again. I was there to ask him for a job, again. It was about a year after the first time I had been to see Bill to do the same thing. I thought it might be worth another shot, and frankly, I had nothing to lose in making the case that my point of view would be a good addition to FOX's programming.

Bill is one of the nicest guys you'll ever meet. I would say the same thing about Phil Griffin, the president of MSNBC, who I've also met with to talk about a job, too. I think that they are a lot alike. Neither of them are particularly ideological, like Roger Ailes is, but they direct programming to drive ratings among their targeted ideological audiences. Personally, I would say that kind, compassionate, personable, and caring are all words that describe Bill Shine. I don't think that there is a homophobic bone in his body, in fact, I would say the opposite. I think he's very culturally connected. He gets it, but he also knows his audience, and at the end of the day he's a businessman. His business is about ratings and audience.

The television news business is very competitive. That's especially true now that there are hundreds of channels competing for viewers. Bill explained to me that when they hire people to be on the air, there are offensive hires and defensive hires. Some personalities bring audience with them, while others are hired to keep them from taking their audience to other networks. It's all "us versus them" in pursuit of ratings.

Bill and I also talked for a while about cultural issues, especially gay marriage. I told him that it wouldn't be long before opposition to gay marriage would be viewed as completely unacceptable in America. He disagreed with me and said that he thought it already was unacceptable! Really, he said that in July of 2014. So I asked him why FOX beat the anti-gay culture-war drum so much. I specifically brought up the Duck Dynasty and Mozilla controversies that FOX covered and debated to death in their programming. He told me that it was because of the "OFWGs." Of course I asked him what that meant, and he said, "old, fat, white guys." That's right, that condescending description is how the folks on the inside at FOX refer to their culturally out-of-touch audience. No wonder Todd Starnes still has a job there, I thought.

This really disturbed me. I know a ton of people who work at FOX. Heck, I've even dated guys who work there! I know that most of the people who work there, both on air and behind the scenes, don't agree with the OFWGs in their audience. Now I even knew, based on my meetings with Roger and Bill over the course of several years, that the decision makers knew that they were wrong to hype those issues. They didn't care that it was bad for the conservative movement to continue to show conservatives speaking out with culturally unacceptable positions, because that's what their audience wanted. Their out-of-touch audience wanted FOX to validate them. The conservative movement will never fully evolve if the top conservative media outlet continues to validate and defend views that have become socially unacceptable. FOX damages the team they claim to want to help, and now I knew that they knew it.

The OFWGs are part of that group who watch FOX exclusively. That is why FOX maintains such high ratings. They only turn to FOX, while the rest of us, freethinking normal people, switch channels and gather information from sources across the media spectrum.

Needless to say, I didn't get a job at FOX. Bill told me that he just didn't know how they would use me. How could they use someone who would challenge the backward thinking of editor Todd Starnes that their audience wanted to hear?

After that meeting, Bill was nice enough to give me one television hit to talk about something non-gay related. I had asked him for that because, now that the culture war was over, I felt that I needed to show that I had a broader scope of work than just talking about issues relating to gays.

That TV hit was about the children, economic refugees from Central America, that were streaming over our southern border and being housed in camps in Texas and other border states. It was a humanitarian crisis. Congress and the president had all left town for vacation and to campaign for the 2014 midterms without passing a bill to deal with the crisis. I was one of two commentators in the segment. The other guy, a Democrat, blamed Republicans in Congress for not dealing with the crisis. I blamed both the Republicans and President Obama for walking off the job in a crisis. I said that we don't pay them to campaign for jobs that they aren't doing! I got a lot of great feedback online for speaking the truth during that segment, but I haven't been back on FOX, since I didn't take the opportunity to engage in the "us versus them" fight and attack Obama while defending Republicans.

It wasn't long after that that I saw a clip from FOX's *Hannity Show*. Sean Hannity was interviewing *Duck Dynasty's* Phil Peterson about his views on politics and foreign affairs. That just confirmed everything we had discussed when I met with Bill.

I was hopeful in 2014 when Christopher Ruddy, the CEO of the prominent conservative media organization Newsmax, announced that he was a creating a new news television channel. He described NewsmaxTV as a "kinder, gentler" version of FOX News. I thought that maybe it would be a place where a right-of-center perspective could be presented without all of the far-right culture-warrior foolishness that was a mainstay at FOX.

The Newsmax news site had been around for a long time, and they had a reputation of being really hardcore right wing, but they were new to television, and they created the impression that they were going to be more thoughtful and present a broader variety of opinions. I hoped, at first, to eventually be a part of his new venture in some way, either on or off camera. I did end up appearing on their network a few times in the early days when they were mostly just streaming content online. They eventually ended up on a few cable systems, but not widely distributed.

I found that Ruddy's talk wasn't backed up with actions. His staff was mostly made up of former mid-market conservative talk radio producers, who produced shows that were just like predictable mid-market conservative talk radio, except with a camera. They weren't as professional, thoughtful, or, frankly, as smart as the production people at FOX. They just couldn't seem to get their minds out of the traditional right-wing radio programming mindset.

One of the worst experiences I had with NewsmaxTV happened when I joined one of their programs via Skype in the summer of 2014. I was booked to discuss the decision by parade organizers to allow a gay group to march in the New York City St. Patrick's Day Parade. The decision came after years of controversy and a long discussion in the Catholic community and the church's archdioceses in New York. I thought the segment was going to be a thoughtful discussion about the Catholic Church's evolution and Pope Francis's new tone toward gays, with the acceptance of gays in the parade as an example of it. That's what I had explicitly told the producers that I was willing to discuss. That's not what the segment was about. I was asked if the gay group that was marching in the parade, the NBC gay employees' organization, would act as if it were a gay pride parade. Would the gays wear leather G-strings and feather boas and act outrageous? Really. After I had explicitly told them that I didn't want to debate a crazy person with an outside-the-mainstream opinion, I was confronted with this line of questioning.

I was furious, but more than that, it was so telling. It was telling that a national cable news network that catered to conservatives would have a host and another guest on who would present that point of view as legitimate. No normal person would think that a gay group would do anything other than treat it as what it was: a St. Patrick's Day parade. They would probably wear green. I haven't appeared on NewsmaxTV since.

More recently, both FOX and NewsmaxTV have turned up the volume on the culture-wars programming with their extensive coverage of the anti-gay industry's effort to rebrand anti-gay discrimination as "religious liberty." FOX's Todd Starnes and Erick Erickson, and former FOX personalities Mike Huckabee, Ben Carson, and Rick Santorum have led the charge to help anti-gay discriminators play the victim when they face economic or public relations consequences for their religion-based bigotry.

The conservative media has so hyped victimhood and stoked fears on the right that conservatives think they have no choice but to pass laws to legalize their ability to hide behind their religion to discriminate against gay people. That's what happened in Indiana with the pro-discrimination, religious liberty law that blew up in the face of Governor Mike Pence. That whole situation was a direct result of FOX and other conservative media ratcheting up the fear and emotions among the anti-gay crowd. The problem for them is that they are the only ones watching FOX News. The rest of America gets their information from other sources, and we have determined that discrimination for any reason is wrong. They are wrong. Unfortunately for the conservative movement and the Republican Party, FOX validates them and gives them a safe place to be wrong, so they'll never learn to see things from another perspective. There's no hope for them.

Most Americans are tired of the current news/talk industry. Their frustration with the two-party system is played out in the programming presented in the media every day. They want more thoughtful, informative programs that feature freethinking normal people discussing the issues of the day, rather than just two sides fighting about which team is right.

Unfortunately, there are still forces in the media and structural problems in our electoral system that preserve the Republican-Democrat duopoly on our national political dialogue and our government. Now it's time for normal people to join together to demand changes, so that everyone's views are represented in our system.

14

NORMAL PEOPLE

Normal people make up the majority of this country. Normal people aren't partisans, but we are engaged and we care deeply about our country. What are normal people, and all the others who don't identify with a party, supposed to do? In our two-party controlled system, it can feel as though normal people like me have no options. How can our point of view be represented in our public dialogue? And it's not just people who look at things the way many people like me do; there are lots of diverse points of view that are not represented in our current system.

More and more people are coming to the conclusion that neither party represents them. Today, the largest group of us are finding our political independence. According to a 2015 Gallup poll, 43 percent of Americans identify as independent. Now, the number of us who are freethinkers and don't want to be team players has grown to the point of critical mass, when we have the ability to band together to fundamentally change the system. It's now possible to finally overwhelm the power of the two parties and reform the process to allow more points of view to be represented.

One of the most encouraging political developments since I've left the GOP was the rise of credible independent candidates in state and federal races in the midterm elections in 2014. An independent candidate, Bill Walker, beat an incumbent Republican to be elected governor of Alaska, and while two independent US Senate candidates, Greg Orman in Kansas and Larry Pressler in South Dakota, were not successful, they did mount credible challenges to the established major party candidates. That's a step in the right direction toward a political world where everyone is able to build a brand of their own and do what they think is right, without the baggage or obligations of being loyal to a political party.

So often, it's the politician's team that drags them down. When the party brand overshadows the politician, there's little hope that the political figure will do more than compromise their principles and toe the party line. It's gotten to the point in Washington, especially, that loyalty to the team is the number one priority. That used to be a key consideration for me in my effort to move the team in one area: I had to be on board with the team playbook to have credibility among the others, because that was most important to them.

This newfound independence is part of a fundamental political recalibration that's happening in America now, where the old labels of conservative, liberal, moderate, and Republican and Democrat don't mean what they have meant in the past. As our broken two-party system has devolved from a debate over ideas into a fight over who is in charge, more and more Americans are walking away from the parties and charting their own political paths. The problem is that the two parties make all the rules to ensure that they are the only ones in power, so it's hard to find your own political path and make an impact.

Too often in our broken two-party system, where only two points of view are represented, liberals propose a big government-based solution to a problem, then the conservatives oppose the liberal solution because it's fiscally irresponsible, then the debate usually ends there. The national organization No Labels has the admirable goal of getting Republicans and Democrats to put aside party politics to come together to solve our nation's most pressing problems. No Labels' national spokespeople and high-profile partners have included well-known moderate politicians such as former Senator Joe Lieberman, former Governor John Huntsman, Senator Joe Manchin, and others.

While No Labels' goals are admirable, getting the current players in the game to focus on working together misses the fundamental need to change the game, not just change the way it's played. We need free-market reforms to the system that will open up the process to more people; that way more people can participate without having to compromise themselves just to fit into one team or the other.

Republicans and Democrats seem to only support free-market election reforms that would benefit their own parties. Republicans want a free market in campaign finance, because they know that they can raise more money than the Democrats if their donors are allowed to give unlimited amounts. Democrats support making voting easier, because they know that more Americans identify with their brand than the GOP's, so more voters likely means more votes for them. Neither party supports reforms in the rules concerning ballot access so that more independent candidates can get on the ballot to challenge them. In other words, they make the rules, and they only support new rules that strengthen their lock on the system. The first concrete action we can take in the public arena to weaken their power is for freethinking people to leave the ranks of the major parties to weaken their strength in numbers. Then we can fight to make sure our points of view have access to the system.

The most promising free-market election reforms that we should consider implementing in this country include making all elections nonpartisan and having open primaries where the top two or three candidates advance to the general election. Allowing candidates to gather the required petition signatures to gain access to the ballot online would be a modern way to reduce the cost of ballot access for candidates. We should also consider ranked-choice voting, where voters give candidates weighted votes based on their order of preference, so that a candidate who is "acceptable" to the most voters, by being one of their top choices, could emerge as the winner. We should consider any number of other innovative reforms to the process that will allow more freethinkers a chance to be viable candidates in elections. I don't think any reasonable reform proposal should be off the table. Americans are innovators, and it's time to bring innovative reforms to the process. Doing the same things we've always done before, even when they don't work, has never been an acceptable path in our country anyway.

Many are already out there advocating for free-market reforms to open up the political process to more players. There is a coalition, led by an organization called Change the Rule, that is advocating for reforms to the Presidential Commission on Debates. The Commission on Debates was formed in the 1980s by the two major parties to organize the televised presidential debates, a task that had previously been done by the nonpartisan League of Women Voters. The Presidential Commission on Debates is made up of an equal number Republicans and Democrats who work together to preserve their status as the only likely parties whose candidates will reach the threshold that they set to qualify for inclusion in the debates. The last time that a third-party candidate has been included in the debates was back in 1992, when Ross Perot was able to meet the high standards for inclusion.

Every four years there are dozens of candidates for president, but most of them remain unknown to the vast majority of Americans because of their lack of exposure in the national media and their exclusion from the televised presidential debates. The Republican and Democratic presidential primary debates often have many candidates on the stage. In 2012, the Republicans had a ton of candidates who were included in the debates. There's no reason why the debates in the general election can't include more points of view. There are credible independent candidates who represent the views of our new majority of voters who don't identify with either major party, but most voters don't even know about those candidates because they can't get into the debates.

Former Presidential Debates Commission member Congressman John Lewis (D-GA) recognizes the problem. Lewis once said, "The two major parties are becoming too much alike, and the American people know it. They want more choices. Maybe if we let people in the debates people will start believing that politics matter." I agree with Congressman Lewis. Both parties are committed to preserving their power.

In 2012, an organization that advocates for reforms to the political system, Free & Equal, whose slogan is "More Voices, More Choices," hosted a debate for all of the minor party presidential candidates. That debate took place on one of the lowest rated cable news networks, Al Jazeera America. In the 2012 election, almost 2.4 million voters cast their ballots for minor party candidates for president. That was a 17 percent increase over the 2008 election. Just imagine if that debate had been televised on one of the major broadcast networks. People would have been able to see that they had real options with candidates who more closely matched their views.

It's been interesting to see the political recalibration that's occurring in the United Kingdom. There are things that we can learn from our friends across the Atlantic. It wasn't that long ago that the only major forces in their system were the Conservative and Labour Parties. Now there are many more choices for UK voters. In their 2015 general election debates, the leaders of seven political parties participated. That would have been unheard of a generation ago. Just imagine if the nominees of seven political parties, or seven unaffiliated candidates, presented their visions for the future of our country on broadcast television. More voices and more points of view will result in more possible solutions to our problems, and that can only help to make our country better.

Free-market-based election reforms, including ballot access, voting, and debates, are important for all of us to join together to advocate for, but there are some other things we can do individually to help change the culture of politics.

The reason that entire political movements can be seen as out of touch is because of our "us versus them" culture in the political sphere. Everyone on our side thinks one thing, so their side thinks the opposite. Then we fall in line like sheep to follow the leader, even when we aren't always 100 percent in agreement with our team. We divide into our separate herds. Then we fight about it.

I am not the only one who hid my feelings of disagreement to be a team player. Too many times when we are trying to fit in we keep our unpopular views to ourselves so as not to upset the other sheep in our pen. Of course, when we have a point of view that we think the other sheep will respond well to, we go "BAAAAAH BAAAAH BAAAAAH" at the top of our lungs! That way the others will know that we belong with the flock.

The most important things that all of us normal people can do as individuals to help change the culture of politics is to become politically independent and also to become outspoken freethinkers. In other words, stop blindly following the people on your team. Making a conscious decision to be a freethinker isn't easy. We are bombarded with outside influences, all day every day. Peer pressure and influence come at us from all directions—media, friends, family, religious communities, political organizations, pop culture—all the different sources of influence on our thinking.

I want to invite you to do a little exercise. Maybe you'll do it for a few days, or maybe it will be something that you continue for the rest of your life. It's something that I do, and it's wonderful.

When you read the news or learn about a new issue, don't look to see what others are saying about it. Just think about it. While hearing others' opinions about things is always helpful in forming our own opinions, try not to do that for a bit. No cable news television or talk radio pundits, no opinion columns in the paper or online. Just read the news and think about it. Make sure you get news and information from a variety of credible sources, not just your usual go-to media outlets.

The next part of the exercise is harder. When forming your opinion on an issue, don't speculate about what other people who you usually agree with might think about it. Everyone does that, even unconsciously. Political people always think about how a message or issue will play to their audience of supporters. Everyone does that to some degree in most areas of their lives. Let's stop doing that, especially when it comes to political issues. Come up with your own position on issues, and don't worry about what anyone might think about you and your views. It's not as easy as you think.

Make a purposeful decision to tune out everyone else. You probably won't realize how much others influence your thinking. Give it a try. See what you really think. The results may surprise you.

Finally, and this is important, don't confuse being a contrarian with being a freethinker. Opposing the popular opinion just to be different isn't always a good idea. Sometimes popular opinion is popular for a good reason—it's right. Contrarian groupthink is still just groupthink, unless you've arrived at that opinion honestly and independently.

Make the conscious effort to be a freethinker, and I predict that you will find yourself agreeing with your usual team a lot, with other teams more often than you expect, and you will probably even find that you have opinions that are uniquely your own!

After all that I went through to try to help to move the entire team of Republicans culturally, I am much happier and productive focusing on being a normal person who just wants to make our country better. I hope other freethinking normal people will join me to work to reform the system so that all of our diverse opinions, cultures, and backgrounds are represented in our political system.

Changing our politics won't happen unless we all take action. The first step is to abandon the broken two-party system. Do it.

Then let's get to work to make our country's political process include everyone, those with a party or those with no party. To quote Harvey Milk, "Let's give them hope!"

Join our movement at www.NormalNation.org.

ACKNOWLEDGMENTS

When I finished the first draft of my manuscript and sent it to my editor Krishan Trotman at Skyhorse Publishing, one of her comments after reading was, "There isn't another book quite like this." This book is kind of outside the typical political-book box, just like most of my career. I can't thank Krishan and publisher Tony Lyons at Skyhorse enough for seeing my vision for it and taking a chance on it, and Krishan for helping my vision to become reality.

My agent Christopher Rhodes, with the James Fitzgerald Agency, worked his ass off to find a publisher for this project. He and I endured a roller coaster of talks with editors and publishers who loved my ideas and the story, but just didn't have it in them to take a risk on it. Thanks, Christopher, for guiding me through that process.

Thank you to all of the people I've met in my work in politics, including those few mentioned by name in this book and the many others—even the nasty bigots. Without my experiences with you, I would not have been motivated to engage in the fight and to write this book.

GOProud was supported by thousands of gay and straight conservatives across the country. Words cannot express the amount of gratitude I have in my heart for you. Thank you. You all know who you are.

Thank you, again, to Chris Barron who gave me his blessing to tell the story about our work together without any input from him at all.

My friends Mack McKelvey and Shannon Chatlos are the ones who coined the very technical political term "normal people." Thanks for letting me steal it!

I'm very grateful to Bill Lacy and the staff at the Robert J. Dole Institute of Politics at the University of Kansas, where I served as a Dole Fellow while writing most of this book. That was the perfect work situation that allowed me commuting time on the plane to write.

Jon Fortin, thank you for letting me take over your dining room table with papers and a printer while I wrote. You're the best, Jon!

The most important thank you is to my family. They went above and beyond the call of duty to make it possible for me to take the time to write a book. Thank you.